What NOT To Do When You Win the Lottery!

How to Manage Sudden Wealth

Angel Love, AFC®

From The Create Your Money Series
Volume II

White Pillow Palace Publications
Fairfax, Virginia

White Pillow Palace Publications
Fairfax, Virginia

ISBN-13: 978-0692737972
ISBN-10: 0692737979

Library of Congress information available upon request

Dedication

This book is dedicated to my children Mercedes, Paul and Jason, and to my parents Eddie and Allie.

Thank you for your unwavering support of me.

This book is also dedicated to everyone who has ever had a dollar and a dream.

Acknowledgments

The second book in the Create Your Money Series could not have been possible without the help of my village… a heartfelt "thank you" to each and every one of you for your encouragement and contributions to this work. Some of you sent an article you thought I might like to see; others invited me to put the books down and get out of the house for a little while. Your love, kindness and positive energy inspire me and I could never do any of this without you.

Extra special thanks to my brother, Mr. Muhammad Bilal and to my classmate at Georgetown University, Ms. Paula Pass for sharing your expertise on this project. A warm thank you to Ms. Mercedes Pettiford for my hair and make-up on the cover shot, and to Mr. Antwon Maxwell for his cover photography. To my editors who graciously gave their time to this project, Ms. Jeanetta Bryant and Ms. Adrienne Washington…. Thank you from the bottom of my heart for making sure my "slip" wasn't showing and for coming through for me.

Table of Contents

Chapter 1: Why Would a Financial Counselor Write a Book About the Lottery?

I remember growing up in New York City in 1982, when there was a lot of excitement around a man named Curtis Sharp who won $5.6 million dollars in the New York State lottery. Word of his good fortune spread all around NYC. Curtis was an air-conditioning mechanic who looked like the rest of the men in our working-class neighborhood, but "just like that," his fortunes changed overnight and he became rich and famous! All of our neighbors talked about his win. If it could happen for him, it could happen for anyone. Curtis Sharp's smiling face was splashed all across the pages of the local newspapers and national magazines. Every time you turned on the TV, there he was smiling and wearing his trademark black bowler hat!

As the days went by, juicy details began to emerge about Curtis Sharp's personal life. Apparently the very colorful smiling man with the distinguished bowler derby had **both** a wife **and** a girlfriend. He even showed up to claim his winnings with both women smiling and hanging off of his arms! Cameras flashing everywhere; he was in the process of divorcing his wife and marrying his live-in girlfriend. He pledged financial support for both women, along with the rest of his family. Curtis had such a magnetic personality, he became the pitchman for the New York State Lottery commercials on TV and was photographed everywhere with celebrities. I was a teenager back then and knew $5 million was enough to seriously change someone's life. I wondered what Curtis Sharp was going to do with all of that money?

Today, Curtis Sharp is a Baptist minister living in a modest house in Tennessee. He still wears his famous bowler hat and he is still known as one of the most famous lottery winners in the country, but there is **no** evidence of the lavish lifestyle he once led. Curtis lives on his social security and retirement checks. He earned a pension during those years he worked as an air-conditioning mechanic, a job he wisely kept for 8 years after he won the lottery. All of his lottery winnings disappeared many years ago. Mr. Sharp spent all of his money buying flashy cars, big houses, giving family members generous handouts and living the " Lifestyles of the Rich and Famous" (a popular TV show back in the day). Curtis also lost a lot of cash making bad investment deals, such as tax shelters that turned out to be bogus. Before he knew it, Curtis was in over his head with debt and the IRS was seizing his lottery checks. It's been reported that he sometimes borrows money from his first wife; the girlfriend who became wife number two is long gone. Through it all, Curtis Sharp is still smiling and he's now happily married to his third wife.

I am an Accredited Financial Counselor® and I work with folks in a variety of financial situations. Some clients are high net-worth, with sizeable assets and estates. Others are barely making ends meet, living from paycheck-to-paycheck. Still others are somewhere in between the two extremes. Over the years, I've had quite a few clients who *suddenly* came into money. Some received inheritances from deceased relatives, won lump sums through lawsuit settlements and a few won the lottery. There were folks who had just begun to receive royalty checks from oil wells on their families' property. Others have managed to save thousands of dollars while stationed overseas. All of them had questions about what to do with their newfound wealth.

Winning the lottery is a popular dream in the United States. People spend hours picking numbers and lots of money buying lottery tickets in the hopes that they can one day win the big jackpot and change their lives. Dreams of mega-jackpots in their heads, folks decide that getting just the right combination of 6 numbers will change their lives forever. All of their bills will be paid, they will be out of debt and they can finally buy the homes and cars they've always dreamed of. They think the whole wide world will be *A-OK*.

There is a popular story about a young woman in North Carolina who was the sole winner of a $188-million-dollar jackpot. The single mother of four children, she took home a lump sum of $127 million in February 2015. She showed up to the press conference with her financial advisor in tow and spoke of her plans to secure her children's future. Holding the press conference was the first indication that maybe she hadn't thought things out as well as it appeared. A few months later it was reported that she bailed her boyfriend out of jail to the tune of $9 million dollars. She posted a bond of $3 million the first time, and another for $6 million after he was arrested a second time. Just before this book was published, it was reported that she bailed him out a third time, spending a grand total of $21 million of her lottery winnings to bail her man out of jail.

There are versions of this story that the media will never tell, and some of the details will never be released publicly. The owner of an executive protection firm in North Carolina recently had the opportunity to work with the young lottery winner. Due to confidentiality agreements he could not tell me much, but he did warn me that her story will play out in the national media soon. Things are not always as they appear, so we must be careful before we judge others. There is much debate in the court of public opinion about how long she will be able to hold on to her winnings if she keeps going down this same path. While the jury is still out, a more important question most people should be asking is: What would **you** do if you won the lottery?

There are a ton of articles on the internet with titles like: "10 Things to Do When You Win the Lottery" and "The First 5 Things to Do When You Hit the Lottery". People tell me all the time, "As soon as I hit the lottery, I'm coming to see you to figure out what to do with my money." If you're coming to see me *after* you won the lottery, you may be "a day late and a dollar short" as the old expression goes. I wrote this book to help folks think beyond their current reality and the limitations of their bank accounts. I want to explore the possibilities with you *far before* you ever come into a sudden windfall. I'm going to talk about many issues that you may have never considered so that when, and if it ever happens to you, you'll be ready to "move-out" with a battle plan.

After reading this book you are going to know exactly *what* to do when you win the lottery. You will know *how* to do it, *when* to do it, and *why* you're doing *what* you're doing. You will know how to keep and grow your money. You will know how to protect yourself and your family. Having a battle plan and knowing what to do empowers you to make wiser decisions if ever you "come into money". We are going to look at winning the lottery from a financial perspective, but we're also going to consider the practical, religious, spiritual, and psychological implications of winning 'big' money.

This book is for Everyone. Sudden wealth doesn't always mean winning a huge lottery jackpot. Sudden wealth could come from a sizeable lawsuit settlement, a life insurance payout, a hefty inheritance, a signing bonus (think professional athletes and entertainers), taking a lump-sum distribution of retirement benefits or winning a huge settlement in a divorce decree. Folks that have a job making good money should read this book. People with talent, special skills or abilities that could be successfully monetized should read this. In fact, this book is for everyone who has something someone else wants, particularly as it relates to money.

Chapter 2: Realistically and Statistically Speaking

Statistically, what are your chances of winning the lottery? Studies have shown that you stand a greater chance of being struck by lightning than of winning the lottery. Powerball is a popular lottery game played weekly in most of the United States. Mathematician, Ronald Wasserstein published a blog in the Huffington Post where he estimated that the chances of winning Powerball was 1 in 175,000,000! A lottery player can choose 5 different numbers between 1 and 59 which could yield over 5 million different combinations. The game also lets you choose a Powerball number between 1 and 35, in addition to the other 5 numbers selected. Multiply the 35 by the 5 million and you could have over 175,000,000 number combinations... yet only **one** is the winning combination!

The odds of winning a $540 million jackpot in Powerball are 1 in 175 million. The odds of winning the Mega Millions game has been reported at 1 in 258,890,850. The odds are determined by calculating the number combinations, which varies according to the type of game played. The odds of winning the average 6 digit lottery game is 1 in 14 million. To put that in perspective, let's compare that to some other odds. The odds of becoming a movie star is only 1 out of 1. 5 million. You stand a 1 in 10 million chance at becoming President of the United States. The odds of being bitten by a shark are 1 in 11.5 million. The odds of being struck by lightning are 1 in 135,000.

Still, those odds don't deter most folks from playing the lottery. I don't know too many people anxious for a chance to get struck by lightning, or bitten by a shark, but I know plenty of folks who will patiently stand in line, anxious for the chance to buy a lottery ticket. As glamorous as being a movie star seems, I'm just not interested in that type of job. Ditto for becoming the President of the United States. By contrast, I'm super interested in winning some money, and I was never good at statistics in school anyway. There will always be plenty of folks that want to win the lottery. People defy the statistical odds to faithfully play the lottery because it isn't exactly a rational decision.

Whenever jackpots in the lottery games grow to astronomical proportions, I always hear people complaining about how the winner of a $175 million jackpot, only takes home $80 million. I always roll my eyes when I hear this... all the way to the very sides of my eyelids, for two reasons. The person complaining doesn't seem to realize that the lottery winner has defied statistical odds to win the lottery in the first place and they are probably ecstatic about that. People complain as if the lottery game is somehow rigged to cheat the winner out of money, when it's really just basic math, particularly the time value of money.

The Lottery Commission uses mathematical concepts to calculate a jackpot: the time value of money, present value, future value and compound interest. If these terms make little sense to you, no worries. Keep reading. I'm breaking it all down right now. Winners can choose to take their prize money immediately as a lump sum, or they can spread out the payments of the jackpot over 20 or

29 years. The length of the payout depends on the specific rules of the state or type of game being played, but the math impacts how much money the winner takes home.

You've heard the saying "time is money"? Well, the value of money depends on time. **Time value of money** is the most important concept in personal finance. It states that a dollar received today is always worth more than a dollar received tomorrow, because today's dollar can be invested and earn interest and it will be worth more over time. The **present value of money** tells us how much the cash we're going to receive in the future is worth in today's dollars. If you want to know how much money you need to invest now in order to have a specific amount available to you in the future, then you're dealing with a present value of money calculation. The **future value of money** tells us how much the cash we invest today, will be worth tomorrow. What connects the present value of money to the future value of money is the interest rate and the period of time the money has to grow. For example, how many years or months.

The amount of money to be invested is the principal, and the interest is the money the principal earns each year. Over time, both your principal and interest earns money. We call this compound interest: when your money earns money and that money earns more money. Compound interest is the reason you can borrow $3,000 on a credit card and if you only pay the minimum amount due each month, it will take you 20 years to pay off that credit card. The interest you owe the bank is compounding and growing out of control. Ditto for the interest on student loans. When **you owe** someone compound interest it can be hell to repay, but when the bank **owes you** compound interest, and owes you a lot of it.... well that's how you make money and keep money.

So what does all of this have to do with the lottery jackpot? The lottery commission doesn't actually have the amount advertised on the billboards and highway signs in their hands. They have a sum of money to be invested (the present value or discounted value) in their hands. The intent is that the money will be invested and earn compound interest. If the lottery winner is paid in annual installments over 20 or 29 years, eventually they will receive the entire amount advertised as the winning jackpot.

A choice to take the lump sum *now* means the winner gets *less* than the amount advertised as the jackpot. The winner gets the present value of the money, or actual amount of money the lottery commission has on hand and would have invested on the winner's behalf. If the winner takes the present value lump sum and invests the money themselves, over time the winner could earn what would have been received had they taken the annuity.

You only get the advertised jackpot if you choose the annuity option. If you take the lump sum, can you or your financial advisor invest that money yourself and outpace the interest the state lottery commission would have earned? There may also be an option for you to take a partial lump sum payout and get the remainder in an annuity, which can reduce the overall tax bill, but that option varies from, state-to-state. We'll talk about that up ahead.

A jackpot advertised as $100 million is based on the assumption that the person will take $5 million payouts each year, for 20 years. The Lottery Commission will invest a lump sum of about $57,349,500 at 6% interest. This is enough to fund a stream of payments worth $5 million each year for 20 years totaling $100 million. If the winner chooses to take the entire jackpot now, then they only gets what's in the pot now.... the principal, which is $57,349.500. The winner pays federal and state income taxes on that amount and takes home $35 million. If the winner invests that money on his own they could still make about $112 million in 20 years but that's not what usually happens. Typically, the winner ends up losing the entire fortune before the earnings ever have a chance to grow.

One of the first decisions you'll make when you win the lottery is whether to take the payout as a lump sum or as annuity. One of the best ways to answer this question is to examine how you currently handle your money. If you currently live from paycheck to paycheck, chances are you will live from lottery check to lottery check, unless you change some financial behaviors (and reading this book is a great start, so pat yourself on the back). What do you currently do whenever you get a lump sum of money? What do you do with your tax return or settlement money? Do you look up and wonder where it all went? Do you have a plan to account for every penny of the money before you even receive the check?

There are advantages and disadvantages of the decision to take a lump sum versus taking the annuity. You might end up with more money than the advertised jackpot if you take the lump sum and invest it wisely, but there are other factors that can impact that decision. The tax bill might be larger or your investments might not perform as well as expected. The disadvantages of taking the annuity are that the payments are not necessarily adjusted for inflation, depending upon the state where you win the jackpot.

If you carry credit card debt, live paycheck to paycheck, or "rob Peter to pay Paul" as the saying goes, then an annuity might be best for you. If you already have 3-6 months living expenses in reserve, have fully funded your retirement accounts and don't carry any consumer debt, you might be a good candidate to take the lump sum. If you take home $1.25 million after taxes and invest the principal in something that earns just 4% interest, the interest will generate an income of $50,000 a year. A million dollars invested at 6% would yield about $60,000 in interest income each year. The interest on investment income is taxed differently than earned income, but we'll talk more about taxes later.

Bankrate.com estimates 70% of people who receive windfalls of money end up blowing the whole thing within a few years. The shock of winning the lottery can set up a gamut of reactions from intense excitement to panic, guilt and fear. Lottery winners exhibit all sorts of unexplainable, irrational behavior from hoarding the money to giving it all away. We'll talk about the emotional and psychological impacts later in the book.

Chapter 3: Real-Life Examples of What NOT to Do

To figure out what NOT to do when you win the lottery, we only need to look to those who have actually won and made poor decisions. Their examples can serve as cautionary tales of lottery winners who had it *all* and lost it *all*. They may have had the very best intentions in the world and probably thought winning the lottery would solve all of their problems; but for many of them, their problems compounded like interest. The Notorious B.I.G. said it best with his song, "Mo' Money, Mo' Problems," and these lottery winners certainly exemplify that. Their stories were splattered all across the internet, newspapers and television. Documentaries about cursed lottery winners publicized the woes of many of them. Let's take a peek into their lives.

Sharon Tirabassi was a 27-year old single mother of three children who worked as a home health aide caring for the elderly and disabled. She was barely making ends meet between her low-paying job, and the child support she received. She had just gotten off welfare when she won $10 million dollars from the Canadian lottery in 2004. Sharon didn't own a car and had to borrow money to rent a car to drive out to the lottery headquarters and claim her prize. The lottery officials walked her over to a local bank where Sharon deposited the money in two accounts, because it was too much for just one account.

What did she do with her money? A good woman with a good heart, she gave her parents a million dollars and each of her four siblings $500,000. One of her siblings was unhappy with that amount and felt she was entitled to receive more since she was with Sharon on the day she bought the winning ticket (and Sharon gave her more). After a lifetime of never leaving home, Sharon treated friends and family members to many lavish trips to Cancun, California, and the Caribbean. She even gave cash to old friends she hadn't seen in years. Suddenly, everyone was her friend… showing up unannounced and asking for handouts for their projects and loans to solve their problems. A good woman with a good heart who had a rough upbringing, Sharon had a hard time saying no to others in need.

After blowing through a huge wad of cash, Sharon finally met with a financial advisor and put some money away in a trust for her children to claim once they turned 26 years old. She married a local man, each of them bringing three children into the marriage. Together they gave birth to three more, for a total of nine children. They bought a big house, a huge yellow Hummer and a pimped-out royal blue $200,000 Cadillac which she named BabyPhat, after her favorite designer line. Sharon became a stay-at-home "soccer mom," shuttling the kids from all of their activities. She bought designer clothes, threw lavish parties, and took more exotic trips. She bought a few houses and rented them out to those less fortunate at lower-than-market rates, and agreed to pay her babysitters rent for a year. Eventually the lavish spending, lawsuits and the results of bad business decisions took their toll on her fortune. The smartest move she made was to put some of the money in a trust for her six children, who can claim the money when they each reach age 26.

10 years later, Sharon is riding the bus and working part-time to support her children while living in a rented house. Unfortunately, kids pick up their money management skills from their parents, so unless there's been some re-training on what to do with money, the kids are likely to repeat the same financial behaviors as their Mother, possibly running through their trust funds and maybe even borrowing against them before they are of age.

On Christmas Day 2002, **Andrew Jackson Whittaker Jr**. hit the Powerball for a staggering $315 million. At the time it was the largest jackpot won by a single ticket in the United States. President of his own construction firm, Whittaker was reportedly already a millionaire when he won, and chose the cash option of $170 million to receive his payout. After taxes, he pocketed a cool $114 million from the West Virginia lottery.

If ever there was a lottery winner who seemed to be "cursed," it was this man. At first, Andrew used his new fortune to donate millions to charities, build churches and to help out family and friends. He became so overwhelmed by friends, family and complete stranger's requests for money that he turned to alcohol and strip clubs for solace and was arrested for driving under the influence. The constant requests for money and the inability to trust the motives of anyone also took its toll on his wife, daughter and his granddaughter, who was 16 years old at the time of her grandfather's historic win. He showered his granddaughter with lavish gifts and a cash allowance of $2,100 per week.

While parked outside of a strip club in 2003, Andrew's car was broken into and a briefcase holding $545,000 and cashier's checks was stolen. In September 2004, the 18-year old boyfriend of Whittaker's granddaughter Brandy, was found dead on their property. The coroner reported that he died from a lethal combination of oxycodone, methadone and cocaine in his system. In 2004, Whittaker's vehicle was looted again, this time the thieves made off with $200,000; though it was later reported that the money had been recovered. In December 2004, his granddaughter Brandy was found dead on a male friend's property. Although the cause of death had not been determined, cocaine and methadone were found in Brandy's system.

Whittaker's wife divorced him and he was sued by Caesar's Atlantic City for bouncing $1.5 million in checks. In 2009, Whittaker's 42-year old daughter Ginger, the mother of Brandy, was found dead in West Virginia. Within four years, his fortune was gone and he lost his family. Whittaker reportedly told a newspaper, "I wish I had torn that lottery ticket up."

Since we're on the subject of tragedy, have you ever heard of a man named **David Lee Edwards**? David was 58 years old when he died in hospice care in his hometown of Ashland, Kentucky, 12 years after he won the lottery. In 2001, David and three others won a $280 million jackpot. His share of the pot was $41 million and after taxes he took home $27 million. He was unemployed and living with his girlfriend, who was 20 years his junior. A convicted felon with a drug addiction, he was quoted as saying, "I want this money to last for me, for my future wife, for my daughter and future generations."

But *what 'had' happened was….* David bought a beautiful 6,000 square foot $1.5 million mansion in Palm Beach, Florida and another home for $600,000 nearby. He bought a $1.9 million Learjet to go back and forth between his hometown in Kentucky and his Florida mansion, also hiring a personal pilot. He bought three racehorses, a fiber optics company, and a limo business for $4.5 million. He owned a $200,000 Lamborghini and a $90,000 Dodge Viper. At one point he had $1 million worth of vehicles parked in front of his house. The neighbors in his upscale community complained that the front of his house looked like a car dealership. He gave his ex-wife $500,000 and he bought his teenaged daughter Tiffany a $35,000 Hummer golf cart to drive around the neighborhood, because she wasn't old enough to drive legally. He purchased a $78,000 diamond encrusted gold watch and a $159,000 ring. It appeared that David was spending at the rate of $1 million a month- spending $3 million within the first three months of his win, and $12 million within the first year.

Edwards hired a financial advisor and an attorney shortly after he won. The financial advisor reported that if Edwards had followed his advice, he would be earning $85,000 a year for the rest of his life based on the investments that were recommended for him. Instead, David sold off the stocks and bonds that had been invested on his behalf.

Was he aware of the costs to board racehorses that weren't winning, to staff a mansion, pay for jet fuel and maintenance of the plane, and the ongoing property taxes for those houses and cars?

The Broward-Palm Beach New Times reported that David and his wife Shawna contracted hepatitis from the needles they used habitually to take drugs. They were arrested several times for possession of crack cocaine, prescription pills and heroin. It was reported that David threw huge drug parties and that he paid for the funerals of at least four of his friends, who all died of drug overdoses. They ran through the money within five years. By 2006, he had lost every bit of his fortune. He and Shawna were penniless, living in a storage unit contaminated with human feces. Shawna left David and remarried. David died without a dime to his name, owing thousands of dollars to friends. His daughter reported that he didn't even have a life insurance policy and she was left with nothing.

They say greed and fear drive all emotional investing of money. **Tonda Lynn Dickerson** worked at the Waffle House when she won the lottery for $10 million dollars. She refused to split her winnings with her co-workers as they had previously agreed. Instead, she placed her winnings in a corporation and granted family members 51 percent of the stock. Not sure what kind of financial advisor she consulted to do that move, but the corporation was taxed as such and she was hit with a $1,119,347.90 tax bill. While she was able to successfully defend herself in a court of law about splitting the ticket with the co-workers, she could not dodge Uncle Sam and had to pay up.

Suzanne Mullins won $4.2 million in the Virginia lottery in 1993 and chose yearly payouts instead of a lump sum. She went into debt using future payments as collateral for a $200,000 loan. Mullins switched to a lump sum payout but never paid back the debt. Old habits die hard, if you didn't pay your bills on time *before* you won the lottery, you're not necessarily going to pay your bills on time *after* you win the lottery. The loan company took her to court and won a judgment for $154,000, but by then she was "judgment proof", insolvent with no assets to liquidate.

Evelyn Adams won the lottery twice: in 1985 and in 1986. She won a total of $5.4 million from the state of New Jersey but she gambled all of her earnings away in Atlantic City and now she lives in a trailer park.

Billy Bob Harrell Jr. was a Pentecostal preacher working at Home Depot when he won $31 million in 1997. He bought a ranch, six other homes and a few new cars. Unable to say no when people asked for a handout, he later divorced and eventually committed suicide.

Willie Hurt won $3.1 million in the Michigan lottery in 1989. Two years later, he was divorced and lost custody of his children. He was charged with attempted murder and addicted to crack-cocaine. His drug habit was so bad, he spent his entire fortune on it.

Denise Rossi won $1.3 million in California. She left her husband Thomas without a word and filed for divorce. Two years later her husband opened a letter delivered to his new home address in LA. The letter inadvertently, told him about Denise's win. He sued Denise for not disclosing the winnings during the divorce proceedings, and the judge awarded Thomas every cent of the jackpot Denise won.

Janita Lee was a wigmaker from South Korea who won $18 million in 1993, spending it all on charity within 10 years. A reading room at Washington University Law School was named after her and she was a major donor for the Democratic Party. Charitable giving, credit card debt, and some gambling were her undoing. She filed for bankruptcy in 2001.

William Post won the Pennsylvania lottery in 1988 for $16.2 million. He was sued by his ex-girlfriend for a share of the winnings and she won. His brother hired a hit man hoping to inherit some of the winnings. Other relatives constantly begged him for money. Within 1 year he was $1 million in debt and filed for bankruptcy. He now lives on food stamps and a $450 monthly stipend.

In 1990, **Rhoda and Alex Toth** won $13 million in 1990. Within 15 years they were destitute. The couple declared bankruptcy and were accused of tax evasion by the IRS. Alex died before the case went to trial; Rhoda was found guilty of tax evasion and served two years in federal prison.

Chapter 4: Great Examples of What You Should Do

There's much to be said about the power of positive thinking and creative visualization. You can change your life, if you first change your thoughts. For proof, look no further than **Cynthia Stafford** who won $112 million in the California lottery of 2007. Her younger brother died in a car accident several years earlier and she was struggling to raise his five children alone. A strong believer in creative visualization, in January of 2007 she began picturing herself holding a winning lottery check with the numbers "112" followed by a whole lot of zeroes. She wrote the number down and meditated on it every day. She so strongly visualized herself winning that she even pictured the exact blouse she would be wearing on the day that she claimed her lottery winnings. She bought a $2 quick pick lottery ticket and on Mother's Day of 2007 she won the $112,000,000 jackpot! There are pictures of her standing there smiling wearing the blouse she visualized herself wearing when she won!

A positive person always thinking of helping others, Cynthia took a $67 million lump sum payout, which she split with her father and older brother. As hard as Cynthia worked to raise her late brother's children, the state took the children away from her and placed them in foster care. Cynthia's immediate priority after winning the lottery was hiring an attorney to help her regain custody of the children to ensure their future. Like a lot of other lottery winners, she splurged buying two Rolls-Royces and taking a luxurious vacation to Paris, but then she got down to business with her money. Cynthia made a point of funding numerous organizations that encouraged children in the arts. She then set her sights on starting her own film-making company.

Cynthia reached out to billionaire movie-maker David Geffen who advised her on investments and she began the process of setting up her own film-making company. In 2009 she became CEO and Executive Producer of Queen Nefertiti Productions LLC, on a mission to develop positive projects for film and television. One of the top philanthropists in Los Angeles, Cynthia set up a foundation to direct her philanthropic efforts. Cynthia was selected to receive the prestigious "Remarkable Women" award by Lifetime Network, alongside luminaries like Michelle Obama, Hillary Clinton and Maria Shriver. Cynthia is enjoying the fruits of making sound financial decisions that honor her. She sits on the board of directors of the Geffen Theatre and has donated over $1 million to the Geffen Playhouse. She has the freedom of being able to create whatever she wants, and she remains humble and full of gratitude for the good fortune she finds herself in.

Not much has been written about **Byron Woods** who was working as a diesel mechanic in July 2003. While picking up his wife Barbara from her job at a convenience store, she reluctantly sold him $5 worth of Quick Pick lottery tickets. The next morning, they discovered they won $49 million in the Texas lottery. The Woods chose the annuity, taking home a check for $2.9 million with $1.95 million to be paid annually over 24 years. Two months after they won, Barbara suffered a stroke, impacting her speech and health. The couple's strong faith in God and family has kept their marriage together for 17 years and they seem to be enjoying their prosperity, taking vacations to Las Vegas and managing their business investments.

Later, Barbara had an idea. The Tee-Pee Motel, located in Wharton, Texas, was known to have a legendary history. Willie Nelson, Dolly Parton and Elvis Presley were once guests in years past, but the reservation had become rundown and long-forgotten. In 2004, at his wife's urging, Byron bought the property for $60,000 and renovated it for $1.6 million dollars. They turned it into a popular RV park and restored the glory of the 10 adobe-style tee pees on the reservation. Today, the hotel stands as just one of three tee-pee style hotels of its kind in the United States. It was important to the Woods to have a piece of Texas history. Byron personally manages the property himself, even though he lives about 65 miles away from the motel on a ranch. He prefers to be "hands- on" with his investments which include real estate, a gourmet coffee shop and several other businesses.

"If only I could win the lottery for a million dollars" or "I just need a million dollars to change my life around" is a common sentiment I hear expressed often. So far, this book has highlighted people who've won several millions dollars. Let's take a look at a man who won just $1 million. **Yancy Hicks** was a manager at McDonalds for 26 years when he won $1 million dollars in the 2008 Illinois state lottery. He continued working at McDonald's for another 4 months after his win, while researching fast food establishments that he could own for himself. He had always dreamed that he would one day open a Subway sandwich shop, so he used his lottery winnings to do just that. After researching the franchise, he made the decision to buy. Yancy paid his daughter's college tuition and bought a home. His only splurge was a $30,000 Corvette. He intended to use the money as a foundation to build on which makes him a successful lottery winner. Yancy keeps a low-profile; being sure to maintain his existing circle of close friends and resisting the advances of new people that would try to take advantage of his good fortune.

We don't hear a whole lot of stories about "model" lottery winners. We hear more about the examples of "what not to do" all of the time. Their stories are sensationalized and plastered all over the news as cautionary tales, but we don't hear as much about those that win the lottery and do well with their money. It appears that the most successful winners continue on very much the same way they did before they won the lottery. They keep working at the same jobs or pursue the life-long dreams they've always held. They keep the same circle of friends and family, and for the most part, make the same wise decisions about money they made before they won the lottery. A great indication of how well someone might do after winning the lottery is to look at how well they are handling money right now.

In 1993, **Les Robins** was a junior high school teacher in Wisconsin when his fiancé sent him out on an errand to a local hardware store one day. He stopped at the convenience store and purchased a ticket just hours before the drawing. Moments later he discovered he won $111 million in the Powerball jackpot. It seems that even the most successful lottery winners encounter some sort of difficulty or trouble related to their big win. The difference seems to be in the way that they handle those challenges. Robins ended up in court to legally divide the prize money with his then fiancé and they never married. He later married another woman and built his dream home on the waterfront; but that marriage ended in divorce.

Robins tapped into his life-long passion for teaching children and decided to open a camp to give back to the local Wisconsin children and to help them re-connect with the basics. He used a portion of his winnings to build a 226- acre day camp along Lake Winnebago. Robins spent summers in camp while growing up in Florida and later became a camp counselor himself. 'Camp Winnegator' combines his love of the lake and the University of Florida Gators. The camp has riding stables, a miniature golf course, pools, and a gym. Every summer, local children ages 6-16 get the chance to ride horses, play games, paint pictures and swim in the lake. The connection with nature provides a much needed reprieve from all of the cell phones, video games and computers children have come to expect as normal.

Robin's Family Foundation oversees the camp and Robins can be seen driving around the camp in his old Jeep Cherokee. He serves as a mentor to children and volunteers to coach basketball in Wisconsin and Florida, continuing to do what he loves. He has created a lasting legacy for the children with something that has stood the test of time. It's been reported that Robins had found love again and was preparing to marry. He advises future lottery winners to put a portion of their money into an irrevocable trust for up to three years. By then they ought to have a firm idea about what to do with the money.

Jacki Cisneros was working at a TV news station as the overnight news editor in May of 2010, when she found out that she and her husband Gilbert won the $266-million-dollar jackpot in the state of California. She was on the job working on news stories that night when she learned the winning ticket had been purchased in her neighborhood. She called her husband and asked him to check the 10 Mega Millions lottery tickets he purchased earlier that day while buying dinner for the couple. When she found out one of those tickets was the winning ticket, she immediately kicked into news editor mode and tried to get an "exclusive story" out of her husband about their lottery win! He wisely declined his wife's attempts to get him in front of the news cameras. Jacki settled for a scanned and emailed copy of the winning ticket and reported her news story. Jacki was so dedicated that she was interviewed nationally by some of her colleagues at NBC the next morning and reported that she would stay on the job, even though she won such a huge jackpot, simply because the job made her happy. Gilbert Cisneros had just been laid off 2 weeks prior to winning and was thrilled to know that he wouldn't have to penny-pinch anymore.

Jacki Cisneros went back to work the night after she won because she had no idea what to do with her winnings and didn't want to be any place else other than work. The couple bought their dream house and vacationed in Hawaii. Then, they used $20 million of their winnings to create the Gilbert &

Jacki Cisneros Foundation and the Cisneros Family Endowment, awarding grants and scholarships to deserving Hispanic students who want to go to college. In 2014, they pledged $700,000 to support Latino students in California who participate in the Congressional Hispanic Caucus Institute's Congressional Internship Program. They gave away over $1 million in endowments to Jacki's alma mater, The University of Southern California, Annenberg, for Latino students who major in journalism, and Gilbert's alma mater, George Washington University, for Latino political science students.

Jim and Carolyn McCullar, had been married for 41 years when they won half of a $380-million-dollar jackpot in 2011. During the press conference at the Washington State lottery commission, Jim accepted the check for $190 million and handed it right over to his wife with a kiss saying "I know what to do with the money". He said that he would write checks to his six kids, and donate to charity.

Grounded by their strong faith in God and family, the couple was initially reluctant to come forward because of all the predators and they used police protection to come claim their winnings. Jim announced at the press conference that he had just $8 in his wallet and no plans to squander their new found fortune. He told reporters that he was more interested in leaving a legacy for his children and his children's children, investing the money in such a way that generations of his family would lead comfortable lives.

It could be said that **Gloria McKenzie** is the beneficiary of someone else's kind gesture. A woman was standing in line to buy a lotto ticket in Tampa, Florida when she let Gloria, an 84- year old widow cut in front of her in May of 2013. Gloria purchased a Quick Pick ticket that turned out to be the sole winner of the $590 million Powerball jackpot. Gloria had 60 days to claim her prize but went into seclusion with her son, her attorneys and financial advisors. They took 2 weeks to strategize before claiming her $370 million lump sum, leaving with $278 million after taxes. Neither Gloria, her son, nor her two attorneys spoke with reporters, but released a statement saying she was thankful and blessed to have won such a prize. Her attorneys said that she would not be making any public statements nor would the attorneys be granting any interviews to the media on behalf of their client and just as quickly, Gloria went back into seclusion.

After the news reported that Gloria was the winner, neighbors were especially surprised because she never said anything to anyone about it. They all described her as a very nice and quiet woman who kept to herself. Gloria never returned to live in her $50,000 house after claiming her prize. It was reported that a moving van showed up to claim her belongings. The news reporters even called Gloria's family members back home in Maine and they were also surprised to hear that she won because she hadn't told them yet. Gloria continued to keep the same low-profile after she won the lottery and was spotted shopping at Walmart and going for lunch at a local diner with her son. News outlets reported that she bought a 1.2 million home in a gated community in Florida, but that sightings of her or any of her children are rare. It was reported that Gloria donated $2 million dollars to the high school where she used to teach, back in Maine. The roof needed extensive repairs and two of Gloria's children still have ties to the school. Reporters are referred to McKenzie's lawyers if they have questions and the lawyers don't ever return the phone calls.

Louise White from Newport, Rhode Island was another elderly woman who used common sense and caution in claiming her winnings in February of 2012. The 81-year bought the winning lottery ticket when she went to the store to buy some sherbet for her family to enjoy. She discovered that she had the winning ticket that evening and slept with the signed ticket inside of her Bible until she could get it to her safe deposit box. The sole winner of a $336 million dollar Powerball jackpot, Louise took home a $210-million-dollar lump sum. Her family kept mum about the win and no one knew she was the winner until the press conference was held a month later. She made one public appearance to claim her winnings and spoke briefly, letting the team of attorneys she hired handle the rest of the press conference. Louise established The Rainbow Sherbet Trust for the money (named after the sherbet she brought that day) to protect her privacy. She gave no indication as to her plans for the money other than saying that it would make her family happy.

Sandra Hayes was a 46-year-old social worker for the state of Missouri when she won a $224-million-dollar jackpot with 12 of her co-workers in 2006. A single mother with 2 children at the time, Sandra wanted to keep her job simply because she loved what she did for a living and had sensible, practical plans for her money. Her take of the jackpot divided by the 13 winners was a $6 million lump sum after taxes. It was reported that she used the money to pay off $100,000 in outstanding student loans and a $70,000 mortgage. She met with a financial planner, bought another home, new cars for her family members and took a few vacations. She also donated money to charitable organizations, many helping victims of domestic violence.

Being a lottery winner and trying to hold onto a social service position proved to be difficult. People from all over the office were sending letters, emails and faxes to her personally asking for her financial help. Folks even started showing up to her job to ask for help, making it difficult to differentiate between them and the clients that she served. Some were even bold enough to show up at her home and stand in her driveway asking for money. A "friend" asked for her help in paying off 3 years' worth of back taxes owed on her home. The woman said she would lose her home if the debt wasn't paid. Sandra offered to connect the woman with various agencies who could assist her, but the woman said she had previously applied to those places and been declined. So Sandra did a little checking around of her own. The property tax records for her 'friend's' house listed no back taxes due and that the current taxes were "paid in full". Sandra pointed out the lie and she never heard from the woman again.

Sandra used common sense to learn to adapt to the challenge of managing sudden wealth. She was so overwhelmed with people asking her for money that she published a book called "How Winning the Lottery Changed My Life". She got down to the business of managing her money, putting herself on a budget and monitoring her spending.

Retired, she spends her days writing, cooking, fishing and gardening. Sandra is one of the very few successful lottery winners that have kept a public profile, appearing on reality TV and granting interviews. She continues to stick to her budget; shop for discounts, uses coupons and saves money. She firmly believes that if you were frugal with money before you won the lottery, you'll be frugal afterward. Sandra also learned the value of making new friends and spending time with people that will buy her a drink or take her out without any strings attached. She spends time with folks who don't always expect her to pick up the tab just because she's a lottery winner.

Chapter 5: Figure Out How You Feel About Money

While most of this book is directed towards handling sudden wealth from a practical standpoint, it's important to explore your thoughts about money from a psychological perspective as well as a religious or spiritual point-of-view. Lets take a moment to consider all of the points that may come up if ever you come into sudden wealth.

It is absolutely crucial that you figure out how you really feel about money as well as how you feel about people you perceive as having money. This is true whether you ever come into a sudden windfall or not. Money is very important in most of our lives. Most folks living in the United States got up this morning and either went to work to make money, or went to school to learn the skills to go to work and make money. Others woke up with the thought to manage their investments, which makes money for them. Everyone else is either retired from jobs they've held long-term, too sick or ill to make money, too young to make money, or a con-artist, robber, and/or a thief sitting up trying to figure out how to get their hands on someone else's money.

The most important thing you need to do in anticipation of successfully handling a large windfall is to prepare your mind. If you expect to grow and keep your wealth, you need to make up your mind about how you really feel about having money. Examine your long-held, deeply rooted thoughts about money, and determine if those ideas and beliefs will serve you well when you have much more than you do now.

Money can be defined as a store of value, meaning people can use it now or save it for later. It is a unit of account, giving folks a common base for prices. It is also a medium of exchange, something that folks can use to buy from one another. Prior to most economies using a form of money, folks bartered for goods and services. Someone traded a bunch of chickens for a cow, or exchanged gold for fabric and spices. The bartering system was replaced by money in the form of currency. Money in and of itself has little value. It can be represented in the form of food, beads, metal coins, or a piece of paper with someone's picture on it. What gives money its *value* is the *meaning* assigned to it by the folks who use it when trading it. A line quoted in a famous song about money says, "For a small piece of paper it carries a lot of weight".

The **biggest** question you will have to answer is "how do you define money? " "Why do you want money? " and "What does having a lot of money mean to you? " Many people want more money, because having more money equals financial freedom. The question then becomes: how do you define financial freedom?

Does financial freedom mean not having to go to a job you dislike every day to earn money? Does it mean being able to explore personal interests, or pursue higher education? Does it mean having the freedom to live your life as you please? What does financial freedom look like? Feel like? For some, financial freedom could be as simple as not having to worry about the "check engine" light coming on in the car, or it could mean the ability to purchase a new car every year and never have maintenance issues. For others, financial freedom can mean owning a car and not having to rely on public transportation to get from A to B. For folks like championship boxer Floyd Mayweather, financial freedom can mean the ability to own a fleet of motor vehicles and aircraft. Financial freedom could be as simple as having the means to replace things that are broken instead of having to live with things that don't function properly until you can do better. It can mean never having to worry about restrictions on where you live, what you buy, or how you spend your time due to the costs of things.

Think about what you would do if you could retire and never had to go to work again for another day. What would you do with your time? What would you do with your money? That is how coming into a windfall could impact your life. Start planning now, before you ever win a dime. What are you going to do with a huge sum of money? Write out your plans, practice making decisions now as if you have the money. Become so used to handling money (mentally) that when it manifests, it's actually no big deal for you to make decisions. Wanting money just for the sake of having money may be a recipe for disaster if you've never really thought about what you will do with a lot of money.

One of the best ways to examine how you feel about money is to take a look around you at all of the people that you consider wealthy. How do you feel about people you perceive as having more money than you? We took some time in previous chapters to review folks who have previously won the lottery and how they handled it. Now you take some time and think of all of the people in your life who have money and/or are wealthy. What are your thoughts concerning them?

When you come into a sudden windfall, you should give yourself time to figure out how you feel about wealth and become accustomed to having it. It is advisable to put the money in accounts and not do anything at all for at least a month, ideally a year. Although not touching the money may seem to be a Herculean feat, the idea has merit. It's nice to be able to have enough money to buy a bigger home, but along with bigger homes come higher costs for property taxes, insurance, utilities, maintenance, and repairs. You need to be able to accurately envision yourself successfully handling that money if you're ever going to be able to keep it.

Using pen and paper, or the notes app on your smart device, start writing down exactly what you would do with a large sum of money. Make a concrete plan of who you would call and what you would say to them. What would you have people do to help you manage your newfound wealth? What are some of the things you'd buy with the prize money? Who are some of the charities you'd give to?

People often fantasize about how they will share their lottery winnings with their family members and there's nothing wrong with giving. You just need to be aware of how having money affects others. You also have to know your own motivations for giving money to people. If ever there were a time when you should learn to say "no," it is now.

In my practice, women are especially guilty of "over-giving" when it comes to money. Nurturers by nature, women can turn into a human ATM for their family members and friends. Men are viewed as providers by nature, but I've seen men "over-give" as well. Especially men who are making up for not being there physically for their family during earlier times, men making up for lost-time tend to be overly generous. While most people are happy to give to those that they love, others are overly generous giving *way* past the point where it is harmful to them. Examine your behavior to date. Do you give family members money that should go towards your own bills? If you have to borrow money from the bank or take it off a credit card to loan to a family member, then you don't *have* it to *give*. This pattern of "giving until it hurts" has to end if you ever expect to handle large sums of money responsibly.

A lot of the spiritual guidance that many people hold dear promotes a warped view towards having money. The Bible says, "For the love of money is the root of all evil" and many folks have taken that literally with emphasis on the words "*money is the root of all evil*". Folks go out of their way to prove that they don't "love money" (whatever that means) or even "like" money, especially folks that don't have very much money. Many folks of modest means are suspicious of folks who have money, believing they somehow did something wrong, bad or evil to get their money. Folks misquote Biblical scriptures and mistakenly equate poverty with spirituality or piety. Matthew

8:20 says "Jesus had nowhere to lay his head" and folks incorrectly interpret this to mean that he was poor, had no money, and was basically homeless, and they further interpret this to mean that if you are a true follower of Jesus you should therefore be poor or homeless as well. Nothing could be further from the truth; this is a distorted biblical principle that ensures that folks remain broke.

Ecclesiastes 10:19 says, "Money answers all things". Simply put, money can solve a lot of problems and accomplish a lot of things. Many years ago I heard someone on a late-night PBS special say these words, "If you have a problem that can be solved by money; you don't have a problem. Sickness, death, and the loss of a loved one, those are real problems, because they can't be solved by money, but if you have a problem that can be solved by money all you have to do is get the money, then you can solve the problem". I've met plenty of folks who believe that winning the lottery and having a lot of money will answer all of their problems. The greatest challenge for some is handling the sudden influx of wealth, which can present more problems than it actually solves.

Folks that consider themselves very religious can be most critical in their thoughts about people that have money. Do you believe that pastors, or other spiritual teachers should be monetarily compensated for their efforts? Many people are critical of spiritual leaders who are prosperous. Ministry leaders often exercise talents, skills and abilities outside of ministry to their own church congregation. They write books, compose music, produce plays and conduct speaking engagements, for the benefit of the secular and non-secular world. Yet people are oftentimes critical of those ministers that make money pursuing those interests.

Famous author, Stephen King has published over 60 books selling more than 350 million copies worldwide in his genre. Published reports estimate his net worth at $400 million and no one bats an eyelash about the massive wealth his books and movies afford him. By contrast, charismatic Christian minister, Joyce Meyer has published over 70 best-selling novels, for which she and her ministry have been well compensated. Joyce has a reported net worth of around $8 million, but there is wide-spread criticism from some church folks concerning how she spends her money. There's been wide-spread publicity about some of her extravagant purchases, and many believe it is wrong for her to display her wealth so flagrantly. Folks misquote Biblical scriptures and mistakenly equate poverty with spirituality or piety, so if you are wealthy you are somehow seen as "unholy" in some circles. These attitudes need to be re-examined.

Some view the very act of purchasing a lottery ticket as gambling. They also believe that gambling is a sin and therefore God can't "bless" lottery winners. Do you believe that gambling is a sin, but it's okay for churches to sell raffle tickets? Do you buy church raffle tickets in the hopes of winning a new television, but you're reluctant to play the lottery because you believe playing the lottery is gambling and gambling is a sin against the Lord (yet you're secretly reading this book)?

What if you are the type of person who will give all of your money away? Some people use their money to "love on" other people thinking, "Well I'm blessed to be a blessing to others." While that might be true, if your Higher Power gave you money just to give away to other folks, don't you think He could have just as easily given it straight to His "intended recipients" in the first place, if He really wanted them to have it?

If you believe money is "the root of all evil," then you can rest assured that you won't ever get the chance to find out what having real money can do. Your attitude about money either repels or attracts it to you. If you believe that "money is evil," your under-lying subconscious thoughts about money guarantee that you'll do everything in your power to lose it, or give it away if you ever get it. That kind of thinking has to change before you can deal with real wealth.

What are your thoughts towards tithing and gifting? Most people say they will give money to the church if they win the lottery but ask yourself are you a giver and a tither with what you have right now? How would your giving change after winning the lottery? Will you tithe a large amount annually to the church your family attends, or will you give to different charities, churches or give to whomever the spirit moves you to give?

We are all given the same 24 hours in a day, and most of us spend a great deal of our time either getting money or spending money. In the book *Creative Mind*, Earnest Holmes says "Man works hard to get money, to buy food, to get strength, to work hard to get money, to buy food, to get strength, to work hard to get money." Try to go one day without spending money, or using up a portion of those things which you have already spent money on. It is virtually impossible. You will spend at least one more day living in your home and using up your rent/mortgage payment; one more day of depreciation on the car that you're paying a note on; one more day consuming food that you've already paid for; and one more day grooming, or caring for your body. It is virtually impossible to go one day without spending money or consuming those things for which you have already purchased. It's hugely important to figure out what money means to you.

There's an old saying that "money changes people". I believe that having money doesn't necessarily change people; it just magnifies who you already are as a person. If you were stingy before you had money, you'll be a tightwad after you get it. If you were overly generous before, you'll probably give all your money away after you get it. If you were a jack-ass before, you'll be an even bigger jackass. If you lived paycheck to paycheck before you hit the lottery, then guess what? Without corrective action and changing the way you think about managing money, chances are you'll live lottery-annuity-payout check to lottery-annuity-payout check, after you win.

While money is most often represented in the form of currency, some believe that the energy of money *is* a form of currency with powerful electrical currents and magnetic charges moving through it as it is transacted. Paper money in the U.S. prominently displays dead presidents on greenbacks, but the currency of money is very much alive and electric! Certainly the energy behind the *movement* of money is powerful. Money can be used to save a life or take a life. Others say that *all* matter has energy. Well money *is* matter. While the idea of intangible representation vs. tangible value is debatable, we know for sure that money matters!

Money flows like the currents and people have the power to either attract or repel it based on their actions, thoughts, or both. I remember a relative once saying that he wanted to be remembered as the filthy, rich Uncle. While the term is commonly used, it literally implies that money is dirty. If you think money is dirty, will money be attracted to you or repelled by you? How many times have you washed your hands after handling money because sub-consciously you thought money was dirty, smelly, contaminated and full of germs? If you believe that money is *dirty* and that people who have money are *dirty and cut-throat*, then that's a guarantee that you will never have it. Even if you win the lottery, with that kind of mentality you could never keep the money or make it grow.

What preconceived ideas do you hold about people whom you believe are wealthy? Do you believe that people who have money are liars, cheaters, and thieves who stepped on top of other people to get it? Do you refer to wealthy folks as "*those* big-time people?" Do you refer to places that are classy, or are a bit exclusive as "bourgeoisie?" These may be signs that you consider wealth as something separate from yourself, something *away from* or *outside of* yourself.

Do you feel that people, who inherited wealth, just fell into it and therefore didn't earn it? As long as you consider money to be something other than you or something from which you are separated from, it is a sure sign that you will never have it. If you ever get it, you will not be able to keep it; it would run right through your fingers because you don't believe that you are a part of it and that you should have it. You cannot separate yourself from wealth and have it at the same time. You cannot possess an "us vs. them" mentality when it comes to money and wealth and expect to keep it.

If you despise people who have money and hold them in contempt that is a sign that you will never be able to attract it to yourself. Do you feel that you are inferior to people that have money or that you yourself are not worthy of having money? Do you pander to those you believe have wealth or position, but treat those you think have no money as if they don't matter? Do you use money to fill up the empty-spaces and places in your life? Some people spend money in an effort to over-compensate their feelings of unworthiness. Do you use people who have money to fill up the empty-spaces and places?

Are you the type of person who needs the approval from others to validate yourself and build your self-esteem? The belief that you need others to approve of you can repel money, especially if you feel that people who have money are evil and not nice people. If you really want folks to like you and you hold the belief that folks who have money are evil or not nice, then you might subconsciously repel money believing that having money can make you unattractive or un-likeable to people.

Believe you are deserving of the money. If you don't believe you deserve to have money you will not keep it. Study the Universal Laws and the Law of Attraction. The Universal Laws cannot work effectively through a person who engages in negative habits such as complaining, bitterness, anger, jealously, judgment and strife. A person who wants to manifest money through the Law of Attraction must first become a good recipient. You have to learn how to receive money in order to keep it.

If winning the lottery is your dream, why would you spend most of your time worrying about what you don't have, can't get, or can't use? We attract what we are. If you spend the majority of your time thinking about a thing, then that thing is exactly what you will have.

Years ago I worked in a financial firm where employees often pooled their resources and bought lottery tickets in bulk to increase the chances of a win. At first I was all in because I certainly didn't want to be that odd employee left-out if we ever won; I wanted to share in the good fortune of the group. After a while, I couldn't ignore my reservations about pooling my money with this group. I got quiet and still and began to listen to some of the group member's rumblings. They would grumble and complain about not ever winning anything; saying things like, "Why are we doing this? We're not going to win anyway." It became crystal clear to me that throwing my money in with this group was a losing proposition because they didn't ever **expect** to win and would therefore LOSE every time…and lose big.

Spiritually, this group did not have winning energy, so putting my five bucks in with them was throwing "good money after bad" as the old folks used to say. I once asked some of the guys in the group if they knew where we had to go to claim our prize if we ever won. Sadly, none of them had ever taken the time to even figure out where the local lottery commission building was. I realized then that no one in this group had ever really seen themselves as a winner. The words they spoke informed me that money was actually repulsive to them and I never threw another dime in with their lot. And they never won anything either.

I am cautious or "funny" about where I buy my lottery tickets. If I don't like the energy of a store or a particular clerk at the cash register, I won't buy my ticket there. It's a waste to spend money in a place that doesn't have that winning energy. You should have in your mouth what you want in your life. I am very particular about being around people that whine, moan, bitch and complain. I absolutely, positively cannot *stand* people like that. As they sit there bitching, whining and moaning, I'm wondering why they're wasting their time on this earth complaining and why they feel the need to suck me into their never-ending vortex. They are given the same 24 hours as everyone else, yet what they choose to do with those 24 hours is beyond amazing. Their lives become a self-fulfilling prophecy, partly because they have no gratitude and aren't thankful for one little thing.

Yes, everyone has a bad day every once in a while; but there are people that can **only** see their problems and what is wrong with the world. If you give them two minutes of attention, they want to pull you into that vortex and regurgitate their negative vomit all over you. It is beyond annoying. This kind of person is a sure-fire repellent for success and prosperity. Stay away from this person if you want to attract and keep wealth. If you *are* this person go get some help to maximize your time here on this earth.

You can't spend your time thinking about what you lack and what you don't have and expect to be a prosperous person. If we really are the totality of our thoughts, why not spend our "down-time" visualizing, thinking about, ruminating, and daydreaming about what it would feel like to win the lottery, and what would we do with the jackpot? How would having the extra money change your life for the better? When you realize how powerful your thoughts and words are, you eventually learn to guard every word that comes out of your mouth. Immediately catching yourself if you ever say something that is not consistent with what you want.

I'm really impressed by the lottery winner we read about earlier, who visualized herself into winning $112 million. She repeated affirmations that she would win a huge sum of money and allowed herself to experience the event as if it had already happened. As fantastic as her story may be, have you ever thought about what you would wear on the day that you show up to claim the ticket? Instead of allowing your mind to trail off and re-hash an unpleasant interaction with a co-worker or a loved one, is it possible to switch gears and now spend some time thinking of all the ways that having money can enrich one's life?

Learn to listen to that voice inside of you. Learn to trust your own instinct, trust the vibes. Listening to your inner-voice could lead you to success in picking so-called lucky-numbers, and it could also help you keep and preserve that newfound wealth, practice following your instincts or hunches. Get rid of a get-rich quick mentality. There is no such thing as easy money. While you may have seemingly inherited money overnight without any effort by winning the lottery, there will be **much** effort required to keep this money. To whom much is given, much is required.

If you're not in the habit of already doing so, develop an attitude of gratitude as it relates to money. Learn to appreciate everything that you have and be thankful for the material possessions already under your control. Get serious about learning to manage the resources that you have. If you have difficulty managing $1,000 wisely, then winning $1,000,000 isn't going to make you an overnight Master of Money. Be thankful for what you have and get help to make those resources last longer. Acknowledge your Higher Power, whomever you conceive that to be, as the source of all goodness.

The American Psychological Association has conducted a Harris Poll every year since 2007, and the #1 source of stress for most Americans has consistently been money. Three out of four adults reported that they felt stressed about money, one in four adults said they were extremely stressed about money during the past month. Studies on the number one cause of marital strife have also consistently identified money at the top of the list (more than children, sex, and infidelity). Money, or a lack thereof, is also the number one reason partners stay in abusive relationships.

There is an entire field devoted to the theory of Financial Behavior (or the Psychology of Money). Studies suggest that habits, behavior and emotions have a lot of influence on how we manage money. Financial Psychologists, Dr. Ted Klonz and Dr. Brad Klonz are leaders in this field and their work suggests that we all have "money-scripts" that subconsciously guide our financial behaviors as adults. These doctors work with clients to help them figure out what their money-scripts are, what motivates them and how to find healthier ways to manage money.

A summary of four money-scripts were reported in The Dallas Morning News as follows:

- Money avoidance: "People with this trait believe that money is bad, that rich people are greedy and they don't deserve money."
- Money worship: "These folks are convinced that more money will solve all of their problems, that there will never be enough and that money brings power and happiness."
- Money status: "Status lovers believe that owning the newest and best things confers status."
- Money vigilance: "People with this trait embrace frugality, the importance of saving and discretion, and how much they have or make."

The elder Dr. Klonz stated, "All financial decisions, no matter how self-destructive or self-defeating, make perfect sense once one understands the thoughts, or money scripts that power those decisions." The team also reports that past experiences with money will strongly impact present and future financial behaviors. People that are having financial troubles should identify their particular money script to see how it impacts them. While there is nothing inherently wrong with the money scripts, if the scripts are running unmanaged and unchecked, that could become problematic. Combine that with a sudden windfall of money and that could become a recipe for disaster.

What beliefs about money did you inherit from your parents, teachers, religious leaders, well-meaning friends and society in general? Deal with any thoughts that money is scarce and that there's not enough to go around. Deal with any thoughts that wealthy people did something dirty and under-handed to get money and are therefore not nice people. Deal with any thoughts about being embarrassed to have money. If you grew up poor without any money, deal with any thoughts at being angry at money for not being there when you needed it. Perhaps you grew up with means and money was used to control and hurt people. You still need to deal with your anger towards money. Are you afraid of money? Do you feel that you won't be able to keep money or that you will always lose it? Does money mean happiness to you? Most folks are ecstatic about the idea of winning a huge sum of money. They think having money will change their lives for the better and in some ways it will. The problem is that many people aren't used to handling large sums of money. They become overwhelmed by all of the pressures and demands that come along with having a lot of money and ending up losing it all, which certainly doesn't make one happy.

Prepare in advance of your winning. Get your mind battle-ready to receive large sums of money and *know* what to do to keep it when you get it. Study money now, study how to manage money, study how to maximize money now.... before you ever win a dime.

Chapter 6: Figure out How <u>Other</u> People Feel about <u>Your</u> Money

We discussed in previous chapters how much money influences most of our lives. We talked about the amount of time folks spend trying to get it or keep it. Money is so powerful that it can evoke feelings of envy and jealousy in those who don't have it, especially towards those who do. If ever you win the lottery you would expect those in your inner circle, your closest family members and friends to be very happy for you. Some are going to be genuinely delighted to see something good happen to you. Others are primarily happy because they automatically assume that you are going to share some of your lottery winnings with them. Family members and close friends may view your win as a win for us 'all' and therefore, *their* win.

Again, it's been said that "money changes people". I'm not so sure that money changes people more than it just magnifies who they already are and what was already there, deep down underneath the surface. While having money may not necessarily change people, it could change how people treat *you*. In order to be successful at managing your money you have to prepare yourself and expect people to change how they relate to you. Not everyone will be happy for you.... A lot of people will be *coming for you*, doesn't matter if you sent for them or not... and they all have an idea about, or plan for what you should do with your winnings.

Most people in life can be categorized as either givers or takers. Sometimes we are a little bit of both, and manage to maintain a healthy balance of giving and taking. Most people operate predominately in one extreme or the other. Winning the lottery will inevitably expose all of the takers in your life. People will ask you for money simply because they know you have it. Folks will want to "attach" themselves to your good fortune, trying to get you to partner up with them to invest in their projects or co-sign their dreams…and every other hare-brained scheme they can concoct.

Takers tend to view lottery winners as lucky folks who put no real effort into winning and should therefore share their prize money. Nothing could be further from the truth. While it may seem as if you were randomly chosen to be lucky and win the lottery, you will **certainly** pay the price that comes along with working very hard to try to *keep* your newfound wealth.

Having sudden wealth means you have something that everyone else wants and some folks will view your money as a means for *them* to get rich quickly. Many lottery winners report that the requests for gifts, donations, and loans from family, friends and people they don't even know, are completely overwhelming. Folks will find a way to get you to fork over the cash. They will try to con you out of it, steal it from you, or try to win it away from you.

You might find yourself suddenly vulnerable to lawsuits. For example, an anonymous person accidentally spills a drink on someone else. Usually a profuse apology and maybe an offer to towel off the spilled garment is enough to smooth things over quickly. The offender may even offer dry-cleaning to the person he or she spilled the drink on. The apology may be accepted, all is forgiven and both folks go on about their day. Not so, when people know you just won $350 million in the lottery. That *same* spilled drink could land you in court facing a lawsuit for emotional and physical damages. Some folks will run immediately to the emergency room with their lawyers on speed-dial, in an effort to document the severity of their "burns". When you have money, you can't just get into random arguments with people you meet on the street. It doesn't matter if you're the aggressor or not, people will rush to call law enforcement and record every word uttered in preparation for the lawsuit that will surely come after this encounter.

Many lottery winners have reported that people try to borrow money from them with no intentions of *ever* paying the money back. How many people are in your life right now asking to borrow money from you, knowing they can't (or won't) ever pay you back? How much more do you think these same people will ask of you if ever you won the lottery? Even those you previously thought were good with their money might try to hit you up for a loan simply because you're the only person they know with 'that kind of money'. They too might assume you have plenty of money and therefore, don't *need* to be repaid.

People will try to keep track of how much money you have, what you are spending your money on, and at what rate. Your lottery win will be the most important topic of conversation for many of those around you. Talking about your money may even become an obsession to some people in your circle.

The first thing most people think of when they win the lottery is taking care of family members and close friends, which is all very noble. In fact, family members and friends may expect you to share your wealth and some will mind your financial business more than they mind their *own*. Some will claim "foul or unfair" if one family member believes you've favored another family member over them with your money. No matter how much money you give them, they will believe that you should have given more. Greed is a part of human nature and many folks operate in it, believing they are somehow entitled to have more than you gave them.

You'll have to train some folks to be gracious recipients. When you gift people with money, those closest to you might ask, "Where did this money come from"? "How much money did you actually win"? They'll make comments like, "You must have a lot of money to be able to afford to give me this". Tell them not to worry about how much you have, just receive the blessing you want to share with them. If they press you for more details, tell them to give back the money if they're uncomfortable receiving it "no questions asked". This will train them to accept whatever you give them and stay out of your financial business.

Some people say they want to keep everything the same as it was before they won the lottery. Money changes people, for better or for worse. If you stay in the same position working with the same people you've always worked with, expect the dynamics to change. Some people treat folks with more money than them as if they're special, pandering to them and ass-kissing in an effort to curry favor. Others may become hostile towards a new lottery winner who keeps his day job, resenting a winner for choosing to *still* come to work after winning. Your supervisor may feel that you cannot take direction since you're no longer motivated by the *need* to keep your day job. In addition to your work responsibilities, managing a sizeable jackpot will take a considerable amount of time and may have to become your new "job". It will take you a lot longer than balancing your old bank account and paying your bills used to take.

Different types of people will approach you and it's important to be able to identify a taker or an opportunist. Some folks "ask" just for the sake of asking, they have the mentality of a beggar and feel that you are obligated to give them something. Giving a beggar money is like feeding a dog. They will come back again and again. If you feed a habit, then it becomes the norm. Beggars are conditioned to be dependent upon other people and expect other people to solve their problems for them.

Some people will come to you with very desperate stories coming from a very desperate place and they will view you as their "final answer". Others beg, not because they are desperate, but because they are good at it and make a good living by panhandling. Some will come begging purporting to represent a charity or cause, but in reality they're only representing themselves, trying to get you to part with your money. Some beggars teach their children how to solicit and may send their children to you requesting money or goods.

You will hear their pitch and instantly **know** these children have been coached to tell you these stories in hopes of gaining your sympathy and money. Don't contribute to the delinquency of a minor. If at all possible, turn it into a teaching moment instead.

Give only *if* and *when* it is your choice to give. Do not encourage aggressive, intimidating beggars by rewarding them with money. These folks are not nice people and they don't really appreciate your kindness or generosity. They take kindness for weakness and attempt to milk you for all you are worth. Be discreet in your giving or you will make yourself an easy target, attracting a host of beggars, con artists, money manipulators and thieves.

Remember the saying "give him an inch-he'll take a mile"? Well, growing up in my neighborhood, it was not uncommon to be sent to a neighbor's house to borrow a cup of sugar, a stick of butter, or whatever someone in the middle of a recipe needed. When neighbors borrow and loan amongst each other, they tend to ask for one thing after another...especially if they know you are a giver. I once moved into a brand new town house community and a neighbor knocked on my door to ask if she could borrow *my* curling iron to use in *her hair*. Just two days after I moved in, I was offended that someone I barely knew would knock on my door and ask to borrow such a personal item. I'm pretty sure she didn't even know my first name.

I used to live on a nice cul-de-sac in Georgia where everyone knew each other. We were all first-time homeowners, raising our kids together and came to know each other over the years. There was a lot of borrowing amongst each other… everything from sugar, to soap, to lawn mowers and ladders. The neighbors were also givers… gifting each other with things like cakes, pies, cookies and gifts at Christmastime; even casseroles when neighbors were sick. I then moved to a comfortable neighborhood in Colorado where everyone had a house with a 3-car garage. I noticed that no one **ever** knocked on anyone else's door to ask to borrow **anything**. Folks were simply givers, never askers. Knocking on the door to give a pie, perhaps some candy at Halloween or some other type of gift during the holidays. Now this is not to imply that affluent folks aren't borrowers or takers. Some of these folks might have been deep in debt in order to support their lifestyles. I don't know, I simply noticed that folks didn't "borrow" as much as they had in my previous neighborhoods.

As a lottery winner it's going to be important that you learn the difference between a giver and a taker, a beggar and a professional fundraiser. A friend who expects nothing from you at all, will be genuinely happy with any gift you give them. On the other hand, there are some family members and friends that will **never** feel as though you've given "enough" no matter what you do. You will have to be prepared to deal with the haters, doubters and nay-sayers. Above all, be prepared for those folks who are not givers at all, and are the most extreme and self-serving kind of takers, and fakers - I'm talking about the con artists.

Con artists use lies, secrets, and tricks to manipulate and steal people's money. They take advantage of people's greed, ignorance, kindness or weakness to quickly gain their victims confidence, friendship and trust so that they can take advantage of them. Winning the lottery makes you an **automatic target** to a con artist. Let's spend some time talking about the "red-flags" or signs that you may be dealing with a con artist.

It's important to be 100% aware of your *own* weaknesses, fears and greed that could make you susceptible to a con artist. Con-artists play on your sense of charity, feed off of your fears and manipulate your weaknesses. They target good people with good hearts, and they have a complete lack of conscience about doing so. They play on desperate and greedy folks as well; that's how they're able to operate. A con artist can pick up on your fears, weakness and/or ignorance because they study your profile. As they study their "targets," they're looking for the weakness; the "in" right from the jump. So being self-aware and paying attention to how you feel when you're around certain people is key.

Pay attention to your intuition, your sixth sense, or any hunch you may have about a person. If something about a person just doesn't seem "right" or doesn't agree with your Spirit… honor that feeling. Trust the vibes. When dealing with someone who is deceitful, phony or disingenuous, you can practically see that deceptive spirit about the person. One thing that I've noticed consistently with most con artists and hustling types is that there is an aura, an air about them, a sense of desperation, deception and manipulation that just rests on these types of people. It's in their eyes and there's not anything they can do to hide that. So again, pay attention to your "Spidey-sense" when dealing with folks.

Liars and con artists tend to think that everyone around them is a fool except themselves, and that no one sees through their duplicity. Unfortunately, deception is a garment they wear and no matter how successful they are at conning folks, we can all see that the Emperor is wearing no clothes, if only we just look. Challenge them on their lies and refuse to fall prey to their schemes. There's also a spirit of poverty that seems to follow con-artists no matter how successful they appear to be, which is why they almost never seem to truly prosper from their cons. No matter what they gain, they tend to lose it all.

Con-artists are deceptive to the core. They enjoy taking advantage of other people because it has become an art-form to them. If they told you their true motives "you have something I want, so just give it to me" that would never work, so they use trickery and deceit instead. They get an adrenaline rush out of "conning" people. Con artists play for needs, wants and sometimes for sport.... Sometimes cons even try to con other cons. They often have a complete lack of conscience, no empathy at all for their victim. Like a sociopath, con-artists don't feel sorry for what they're doing or have done to you. They believe that you "deserve" to be taken advantage of and that somehow you asked for it.

What do con artists look like when they show up? Well it all depends. A con artist excels at looking like or being whomever it is they need to be, in order to get what they want. They show up in your life and make themselves seem to be the "answer to your prayers." Romantic con artists seem to be just what you've *been dreaming of.* They do this by profiling and studying their victims to uncover vulnerabilities. They do this with intense focus, as if their very life depends on it because in a sense, it does. They are excellent listeners and very good at "reading" people. They will figure out what motivates you, what moves you. They may hone in on your sense of pride, ego, illness or your fears. They quickly tap into your emotions to see if you are motivated by greed or a need for love, and then play on your insecurities.

Con artists will go out of their way to study families and the dynamics between family members, looking to see who they can get close to. They work hard to blend in with a chameleon-like ability. Con artists attempt to dress like their victims, speak the victim's professional jargon, or seem to live the same type of lifestyle as the victim. If the victim is religious, you'll find them all of a sudden going to church and talking about "Praise the Lord!" If the victim belongs to the country club, you'll find the con artist dressing in preppy clothes and carrying golf clubs. They can assume a business persona if necessary, or that of a trusted confidante or friend.

A con artist will stop at nothing to find you. They have no shame about calling you excessively, tracking you down or even showing up on your doorstep. Once they have identified you as the mark, they'll go out of their way to locate you and gain your confidence… get into your circle. They'll always remember your birthday and never forget things that you say are important to you. Once a con artist gets what they want from you, they move on and limit contact with you. This is the person who calls you every day to check in and "see how you're feeling" until they get what they want from you. Then all of a sudden, you don't hear from them so much.

Con artists operate by building a false sense of trust within people. The quickest way they do this is by making you believe that they trust YOU. They go out of their way to build **'con'**-fidence in their victims, hence the term "con-man". Con artists go out of their way to make it appear that they are the only ones you can really rely on in order to gain your complete trust. Inevitably they will reveal their neediness or seem vulnerable or fragile. They will appeal to your goodness and your sense to help someone in need but it's all an act. Once you lower your guards and begin to trust them ... BAM!

In order to gain your trust, some con artists honor their commitments initially, but eventually they will slack off. You may loan them $1,000 or $2,000 several times and each time they will pay you back in full. That is only to get you to drop your guard so that when they ask you for the $25,000 or $50,000, you will agree. Of course, you'll never see them again… and you will have never seen that coming.

Con artists use flattery to brainwash, manipulate and reel you in if they feel they need to appeal to your pride or ego. Con artists flatter and praise you on a level that is almost uncomfortable. To compliment someone is one thing, to pat someone on the back for a job well done is yet another thing; but flattery goes in a whole other direction. The con is trying to puff you up and make you think that they really like you. They try to make you feel good about yourself and it's not because they're really nice people. Their ulterior motive is to groom you and make you believe that they really like you, so that you'll like them and then they can use you. After all, we trust people we like- don't we? The con-artist is just setting you up so that you'll easily agree with whatever request they're going to hit you with later.

You have to ask yourself, "What is this person's true interest in me"? Why are they flattering me and lavishing all of this attention on me? While you can't walk around suspect of every person you meet, you'll need to pay extra attention to all of the con artists that come out of the woodwork when you come into a windfall of money. Do not give away your trust easily. Again, do a background check. Make sure people are who they say they are. Do your homework, investigate their claims, and their relationships before signing contracts and getting into relationship with them. If your instinct tells you that something isn't right, believe it and cut off contact with that person. Don't give them any more ammunition than they already have.

There are con artists who specialize in business interests and concerns; be it a brick and mortar operation or a business conducted over the Internet. There are cons operating on a street-level and those in the construction, home-building, home-improvement business. A business con artist may appear to be a subject matter expert. They will be well versed in that business and you get a sense that they know their stuff. A con-artist may namedrop and provide detailed credentials and evidence of their experience, but you should never take that stuff at face value. Check, check, and then double-check again.

I read a story about a husband and wife who avoided a business con artist that could have potentially bilked them for hundreds of thousands of dollars, simply by paying attention to details. The couple noticed that the man they were about to enter into a business deal with had a ketchup stain on the white button-down dress shirt he wore underneath his business suit. The stain was just above the man's cuff links and it appeared to be an old stain, the kind that doesn't fully come out in the wash. This called attention to the whole shirt not being as crispy white as someone conducting business on this level would normally wear. The couple followed their instincts, aborted the deal and saved themselves a ton of money when they later found out the con artist was arrested for fraud. He had bilked people out of millions of dollars.

Con artists go out of their way to avoid questioning or shining the spotlight on themselves, so as not to blow their cover. Pay close attention to the inconsistencies and things about their story that just don't add up. Ask questions, and don't allow them to sidestep the issues by accusing you of paranoia or mistrust. Don't allow them to turn the whole thing around on you and blame you for the mistrust and fear they instill in you.

Con artists will often have a sense of urgency to whatever it is that they are asking of you. Whatever favor, money, or deal they're asking you to co-sign is something they'll need "immediately." They will talk about how if you don't sign the deal today you'll miss out, or that they need an answer now or the opportunity will disappear. This is in an effort to get your money and run before you have a chance to figure it all out. Take your time when dealing with folks and don't allow yourself to be pressured. Do your research, consult with other advisors, and ask plenty of questions.

Remember con artists operate on people's own greed, with promises that whatever deal or plan they have is going to be a HUGE deal. To gain your cooperation, they will tell you that if you don't get in on the ground floor of this deal you're going to miss out on thousands, or millions of dollars. They ultimately want you to work for free in support of their vision, or use your money to fund their research and further their project. Of course you'll never see a return on your investment of time, money or resources. It's all fluffy, flowery talk.

Sometimes they try to trick you into secrecy and make you think that by telling someone, it would give another person the advantage over you in the deal. This is all designed to get you not to talk about them to other people that could possibly weigh in as the voice of reason, and get you to second guess, doubt or question their motives. They may even convince you that everyone else around you is lying, even law enforcement. The con-artist will try to foster an "us against them" mentality.

No matter how good a con artist is, most of them can't operate indefinitely without detection. After a while, people get suspicious and catch onto them. This is why con artists tend to move frequently. They have to be constantly on the lookout for "fresh-kill" and they're typically on the run from their last victims that have discovered their motives.

Lastly, there is the most common type of con artist all lottery winners might expect to encounter. It doesn't matter if you're married or not… the romantic con artist. Romantic con artists will tell you that you are The One; you're their soul mate and they are really "feeling" you. They'll tell you they never felt this way about anyone before and you're blowing their mind. All this stuff is to set you up for the trap of gifts, money and favors. They'll set up a situation to make you think they are "here for you" and you can rely on them.

Beware of someone you just met lavishing praise, concern and extra special attention on you, especially if you are lonely. Con artists have a special ability to tap into that need and seemingly meet it. They'll say that all they want to do is take care of you. Run your bath, cook for you, wash your clothes, dress you…. They almost sound like the perfect maid and if you listen carefully you'll wonder when are they going to be working on their *own* visions, dreams and plans if they're doing all of this "taking care of you?"

Old girlfriends and ex-boyfriends will come out of the woodwork when you win the lottery. They will reach out, calling and texting you, trying to reminisce about all the people, places and things the two of you shared together. They will try to set things up for further contact so that they can gain access to your money. They will tell you that the two of you are soul mates that should have never broken up before they give you a sob story about the hard times they have fallen on. Some of these ex-lovers will even be married and their current husbands and wives will help them scheme, telling them exactly what to say to you. The two of them will sit up all night trying to figure out a way to scam you out of your money.

A sad and unfortunate reality is that you simply have to be prepared to see the ugliest side of people if you ever win the lottery or come into sudden wealth. Being armed and equipped beforehand can help you avoid some potential landmines.

Chapter 7: Don't Tell Nobody... Keep Your Mouth Shut and Protect Your Family!

I imagine that the feeling of checking the numbers on your lottery tickets and finding out that you are the winner of a large jackpot must be **amazing**. Joy, unspeakable joy!!! There's probably lots of dancing, and shouting and hugging and crying with all the folks that live in your house! Then there's probably a flurry of excitement as folks are called on the cell phones to share in the good news. Others are running into the streets telling the neighbors about their great exciting news. But none of this is what you want to do.

As soon as you check your numbers and discover you are the winner... LOTTO PLAN ACTIVATES... silence don't tell anyone... not a single soul! Stay anonymous, and go underground. Protect your family while implementing your battle plan. Your life is about to spin 360 degrees. As soon as people know that you've won the lottery, you'll be badgered by requests for money. This is the time to disengage and go to that place of seclusion you already had planned for a moment like this. Keep your privacy for as long as possible. News like this spreads like wildfire throughout the community and becomes the topic of conversation for everyone who knows, or is connected to a lottery winner.

How are you going to claim your money? The moment you win the lottery you have to grapple with a few technical issues involving the ticket. Read the instructions on the back of the ticket carefully. You can also find additional instructions for winners on the state's lottery commission website. A lottery ticket is a bearer instrument. That means anyone in possession of the ticket can sign it and receive payment. It is suggested that you sign your name on the back of the ticket immediately. If you plan on forming a blind trust to accept the money on your behalf, find out if signing your name on the ticket will prohibit you from doing so (we'll talk more about forming a trust up ahead).

You might not want to put the ticket in that big white family Bible on the coffee table. Make color copies of the ticket (front and back) and put the winning ticket in a safe-deposit box at your local bank. If you lose your ticket, you lose your claim to the jackpot. You won't be officially declared the winner of the lottery until you present the winning ticket at the state's lottery commission office.

Martyn and Kay Tott were in the news after winning a $5 million jackpot because they lost the ticket to claim the prize. There was a 30-day time limit on recovering lost lottery tickets so the jackpot remained unclaimed. The Totts reported that the stress of thinking they were going to have all of that money and then having it all taken away was the cruelest torture imaginable.

Depending upon your state, lottery tickets expire anywhere from 90 days to a year after the numbers are drawn. Most states give you six months to claim the winning prize. Use the time before you claim the prize wisely to strategize. Way before you ever win the lottery you should go to the state's lottery website to find instructions on where to go to claim your prize. Figure out how you would get there if ever you won. Some games are played across multiple states such as Mega Millions and Powerball, and you might have to go to the state in which you bought the lottery ticket to claim your winnings. You can contact the lottery office to make an appointment to collect your winnings, but it's advisable that you first speak with your attorney and your financial advisor, as well as plan for the safety and security of your family.

Forty-four states and the District of the Columbia have a lottery, and most state laws prohibit lottery winners from remaining anonymous. Winning the lottery in most states means your name, hometown, amount of money you won, and location where you purchased the lucky ticket become a matter of public record. This serves two main purposes: First, it preserves the integrity of the lottery, preventing claims that the lottery is somehow "rigged and personally benefits the state lottery officials." Second, requiring that the winner be publicly identified is great publicity for the lottery. If people see that an average person can win the lottery, they believe that it's possible for anyone to win- which drives ticket sales. Some states also require winners to: participate in a news conference, publish their photo to the lottery website and release it to other social media.

At the time of this writing just six states allow winners to remain anonymous: Delaware, Kansas, Maryland, North Dakota, Ohio and South Carolina. Winners can mask their identity by choosing legal entities such as a trust, to claim their prize money. Forming a blind trust with your attorney may help you remain anonymous when collecting your money. Colorado, Connecticut and Vermont, allow you to keep your name private only if you collect your winnings through a trust or a limited liability company. Check the laws for the state where you purchased the winning lottery ticket, which may not necessarily be the state you live in.

A lottery winner in South Carolina chose to remain anonymous when he collected a $400 million jackpot. The man reportedly danced around his kitchen when he found out he won and didn't tell a soul except his dog. Just because the state allows you anonymity doesn't mean you're in the clear. Folks in your inner circle or the news media could "out" you.

While you may have to publicly come forward to claim your prize, there are options to reduce exposure. Several lottery winners in different states have been photographed with the prop over-sized check covering their faces as a way to conceal their identity. It's a good idea to say as little as possible when you attend the state's press conference. Some winners choose to say nothing more than that they are grateful and thank you. This is not the time for sharing all of your hopes, dreams and plans with the world.

The media will publish the names of winners and go to great lengths to interview either the winners or people that know the winners. By coming forward to claim the prize money you open yourself up to public scrutiny of your actions and how you spend your money. Family members, friends, co-workers, acquaintances and people who don't even know you will want to reach out to you. Some want to shake your hands to wish you well, others in hope that your good fortune rubs off on them. Of course there are the con-artists and all of the other folks you can expect to come out of the woodworks. This is why silence on your part is key.

Some people choose not to tell anyone in their family except for their significant others. Others choose not to tell their children, especially younger ones. Little kids tend to brag about everything and this could put them in harms' way. Desperate people who are after your money could even kidnap your children; so your family's safety is of great importance. Also, consider the psychological impact on your children. Will knowing that their parents won a large windfall impact their ability to be motivated to work and/or be productive members of society? What if a parent does everything right but leaves money to children that have not been trained on to manage money?

Since we're talking about signing the ticket and not telling anyone you won the lottery, it's important that we talk about physical safety at this time. In addition to hiring financial and legal professionals, you may have to hire executive protection. The lottery brings sudden wealth but also sudden notoriety, especially if you live in a large city and your face was splashed across all of the media outlets. How do you choose someone to guard your body? There is a big difference between security and executive protection. There's a difference between law enforcement and executive protection. Even though you don't actually leave the lottery headquarters with bags and bags full of money, you *need* executive protection. What is it exactly and what kind do you need?

I spoke with Muhammad Bilal aka Shadow, the Founder of Shadow Protective Services, LLC, a premier executive protection firm headquartered in North Carolina. He provided excellent suggestions for hiring and retaining executive protection after inheriting or winning large sums of money. We discussed several aspects of exclusive protective services that anyone who has something of great value should consider and I am including the verbatim transcript of the interview here:

Whether you claim your winnings anonymously or not, there are a few things you should know and must do to protect your newfound wealth, your family, your loved ones and your assets. Immediately after contacting the appropriate attorney or legal firm, you must contact a reputable protection specialist or protection company.

It is not recommended that you use a security officer, security guard or traditional security company - because you "secure" things and you "protect" people. If you were in a nightclub and a fight broke out, the security will deal with the disturbance by attempting to force the combating parties outside. They may attempt to break up the disturbance, but that's not their primary concern. Their goal is to ensure the security of the establishment. However, if you have a protection specialist, he or she won't care if the club burns down, that's not their concern – the protection specialist is there to protect you from intentional harm, unintentional harm and embarrassment.

Your first step would be to contact your individual state-licensing agency for protection. Many states, which do not have a separate licensing agency for protection, only allow that function to be performed by licensed private investigators. This is not the same as a security guard license. Contact that state licensing agency or professional association, and request a list of the companies that handle high net-worth clients. Do not discuss your wealth with anyone, period. There are reputable companies with client rosters whose net-worth is in the millions and billions. These companies have templates for security threat assessments and contingency plans that they can put in place for your total protection (personal, home & assets). There's no need to re-invent the wheel and blindly choose your own security since there are firms out there that do this for a living.

You don't know what you don't know, and mistakes very early in the game can compound faster than interest and cost you tremendously. Do not hire anyone with military experience only. Yes, there are members in the safety, security & protection community who have military experience; I am one of them. However, if that is their only experience- they are at a tremendous disadvantage. The military viewpoint and the civilian experience are entirely different, and it is extremely difficult to merge the two without conflict.

Do not hire anyone with only law enforcement experience. Some protection details are composed entirely of law enforcement officers but their task, purpose and mission are not the same as your needs. They are primarily protecting government and elected officials. Additionally, there will be certain liability issues to consider when hiring off-duty law enforcement officers for the role of protection specialists.

Do not hire inexperienced friends or family members for your personal protection. If they are employed in the safety, security & protection field by another company, that's different. If they have the required licensing and registration, that's fine. If they have the required insurance, training, experience and assets to accomplish the job- go for it. However, if you had a major medical issue that was possibly life threatening, would you allow a family member or friend to perform the medical procedure? No. You would you seek the best doctors in the world with the best facilities that your money could buy. Well it's the same with the protection industry.

The most common name for a protection specialist is "bodyguard." The specifics of the industry are so much more complex than that title conveys. Unless you're in Europe where that title is revered, the term usually conjures up images of big burly men (and women) with more brawn than brain. And in reality, the safety, security & protection field is so much more.

The most common is an executive protection specialist, but there is also a "celebrity" protection specialist, a "diplomatic" protection specialist, a "very important person" (VIP) protection specialist and a "high net-worth" (HNW) protection specialist. You have to choose the right individual or firm for the specific task at hand. In the lottery states that allow winners to remain anonymous, you would require a HNW or VHNW protection specialist; whereas in another state that requires your identity to be published, you may become an instant media sensation requiring a celebrity protection specialist.

One of the first documents you (and your attorney) should be discussing with a potential protection specialist and/or company is a nondisclosure agreement (NDA). Check to see if they will give you a roster of their previous clients. If they disclose that information to you, just how secure do you think your sensitive information is going to be? Limit your social media profile and exposure, immediately. Contact a security protection specialist that can show you, your family members and loved ones how to limit revealing potentially damaging information online, especially thru social media sites. There are security companies that specialize in managing your affairs in that area and I highly suggest you use them. Posting your success on social media could expose you to scams, blackmail, identity threats and a host of other potential crimes or harmful situations.

To learn more about the executive protection or for a list of private investigators in the various states and regions of the US contact the firm:

Muhammad Bilal (Shadow)
Founder
Shadow Protective Services, LLC
100 Hay Street
Suite 708
Fayetteville, NC 28301
(910) 484-0001 office
(910) 689-8089 weekends & emergencies
e-mail: shadow@sps500.com
Social Media:
Facebook: http://bit.ly/28YOSfh
LinkedIn: www.linkedin.com/pub/muhammad-bilal
Website: www.sps500.com

Chapter 8: Obtain Wise Counsel…Lawyer Up!

You can expect a legion of financial planners, advisors and attorneys to solicit you once you've won the lottery. It's going to be very hard to try to determine who is for you and who is against you. If ever there were a situation in which you'd want to be "lawyered up", showing up financial advisors "deep" … this is it. There are several different types of attorneys and many different types of people who manage money. It is of the utmost importance that you know the differences between the various professional designations, what they are qualified to do, and what their limitations are. You should also know what to consider when hiring these professionals.

Now, before your win, would be a great time to learn what type of people should be on your advisement team. Don't wait until you have the winning lottery ticket in your hand. Armed with your newfound knowledge, you can hand pick your team rather than using a pre-assembled team that someone else in the lottery commission or banking industry has recommended. Now is the time to figure out how each team member functions. Check the backgrounds of professionals you are considering. Carefully vet them and look for people who have a long track record of managing wealth before you consider allowing them to manage your money.

Obtain wise counsel before discussing the specifics of your situation with anyone. If you live in a small town, you may consider finding professionals in nearby larger cities to further protect your anonymity. Managing sudden wealth will become a full-time business and you'll need to assemble a power team to support you. There are three major areas that you'll need to consider: law, taxes, and overall money management. Therefore, your three major players will be: an attorney, a tax professional, and a financial planner. There is also a cast of supporting players you might consider, but these three are your MVPs. While it is possible that one person can specialize in all three areas, if you have more than one specialist, you can maintain complete control and set-up a system making them accountable to each other, as well as to you. This provides a system of checks and balances, so that no one person has all of the power.

You'll need an attorney for a variety of reasons, from helping you navigate the process of claiming your prize, to setting up some serious estate planning to helping you preserve your wealth and pass it on to future generations. Your attorney can also protect you from lawsuits. Coming into a large sum of money makes you an automatic target for lawsuits. People will want to sue you for everything and you'll need a lawyer that can effectively defend you against these kinds of lawsuits, however frivolous they may be.

There are numerous fields of law that attorneys specialize in such as: criminal law, immigration law, malpractice and personal injury. Those best suited to help you handle your newfound wealth would be: estate planning & trust attorneys, family lawyers and tax attorneys. Many lawyers are general practitioners with experience in a variety of legal services, such as divorce, family matters, wills, personal injury, probate, bankruptcy, criminal and real estate law. Others have a narrower focus, specializing in just one area exclusively.

Back in the day, you could thumb through The Yellow Pages to find local attorneys, but would you really want to trust your newfound wealth to a group of well-suited strangers who look good in a group shot? Nowadays, there's a plethora of information available online to help you research attorneys, but filtering through all of it could present a challenge. Many people rely on referrals to find an attorney, but if your circle doesn't include very many wealthy people able to refer you to competent legal representation, how will you find the right one?

The Lawyer Referral Service for your state, county, or city bar association is a great place to start. The American Bar association, www.abalawinfo.org and www.nolo.com are websites that provide answers to general legal questions. Martindale Hubbell is an information services company for the legal profession founded in 1868. They publish a law directory with background information on thousands of lawyers and law firms in the United States. The directory is available online and you can browse lawyers, as well as read both peer and client review ratings at Martindale.com. In addition, Lawyers.com offers directory information on over 1 million lawyers.

Be sure to consult with an attorney who specializes in dealing with estate planning and high net-worth individuals. The American College of Trust and Estate Counsel is a professional organization of lawyers, judges, and law professors specializing in estate planning, trusts, tax law, and estate law at ACTEC.org. You can search their database of attorneys by location and practice. Contact your state bar association to verify their license to practice in your state. Find out if their license to practice law has ever been revoked and if the state bar association has ever disciplined the attorney for any reason.

Interviewing a prospective attorney can be a two-way street. You ask questions of them and they will question you to determine if they're the best type of attorney to serve you. Interviewing each other will help decide if you should enter into a client-lawyer relationship. Ask about their experience in handling high net-worth individuals, particularly those that have recently attained wealth as opposed to clients that have been wealthy for generations. You can ask this without giving away the exact specifics of your particular situation. A successful trial attorney with many years of handling criminal cases will probably not be the attorney best suited to handle your estate planning. Ask if they have any special credentials in this practice and if they're certified as a legal specialist in this practice area.

You will need to be very clear on how they will charge for their services. Ask if they charge a flat fee for a particular service, do they charge by the hour, or will you be required to pay a retainer. A retainer is an advance payment or deposit required at the time you enter into agreement with an attorney. The attorney puts that money in a special trust account and deducts the cost of services from that account, as they accrue. Ask if a retainer is required? As a recent lottery winner you may not have the funds for a retainer immediately available, so ask about your payment options. Ask if they carry malpractice insurance and how much coverage do they carry. Ask how frequently you will be billed. Ask if you will be billed for emails and phone calls to their office, or are you just billed for face-to-face visits.

Ask the attorney for references from past clients. Due to the confidential nature of the attorney-client relationship, the lawyer should not provide you with references without first getting permission from the client to do so. You might expect that high net-worth clients would be less likely to give the lawyer consent to allow them to be questioned as a reference. If you're able to contact former clients, interview those people to assess their experience with the prospective attorney. Did the former client work directly with the attorney or did they communicate more closely with a para-legal from the attorney's office? When the client contacted the attorney through email or by phone, how fast did the attorney return the clients phone call? Did they conduct most business with the attorney remotely or face-to-face?

Winning the lottery can mean suddenly having to figure out who owns the winning ticket and whose name to put property in. Ownership of the winning lottery ticket is impacted by such factors as the marital status of the winner, and if there is more than one lottery winner on the same ticket. How property is titled and whose name assets are in impacts how money is managed, how property gets taxed, and who gets it when the owner passes away.

Married lottery winners should consider their state marital laws concerning ownership of marital property. Community property states consider most property acquired during marriage as equally owned between the spouses. A winning lottery ticket purchased by a married person living in a community property state is considered community property. At the time of this writing there are nine community property states in the United States: Arizona, California, Idaho, Louisiana, Nevada, New Mexico, Texas, Washington and Wisconsin. Alaska is an opt-in state which means it gives married people the option to make their property community property. All of the other states observe the common-law system, which allows spouses to own property separately, in just one spouse's name.

When a person of modest means dies, family members may ask, "did someone have a policy on him" or "did she have life insurance?" This is usually asked to figure out if there is enough money for a decent burial and/or will there be some money left over to help settle final debts and take care of dependents. When a person assumed to be wealthy dies, folks may ask if the deceased had a will, or did they have any trusts set up? This is asked to determine how that money or property is going to be divided up and/or passed on. Probate is a formal process of transferring ownership of assets from a person who has died to others, and it is done through the court system.

Probate law varies from state-to-state and the probate process can be expensive and time-consuming. The process is conducted through the court and details about the case can be made public.

Lawyers, judges and administrators hash out all of the details to ensure that the deceased person's creditors are paid. The courts appraise the deceased estate to determine the total cash value. Taxes are assessed on the decedent's estate, debts are formally settled and property is passed in an orderly, legal fashion. Probate avoids a "free-for-all," with everyone showing up to the decedent's estate and grabbing all the stuff they can because the deceased didn't leave a will. In cases where there is a will, probate is where challenges to the will arise. After that hurdle is passed, clear title to the property can be granted. During the probate process, property may or may not go to the people the deceased intended.

One of the primary reasons people form trusts while they are living is to avoid the probate process after their death. Property placed in the trust transfers to the trust beneficiaries. This provides privacy as to how assets are dispersed when someone dies. Trusts can also protect the privacy and/or anonymity of a lottery winner while they are alive. Putting money into a trust is a way to achieve income, gift, or estate tax savings and it protects assets from the Grantor's creditors.

An estate planning attorney would be the best person to help you set up a trust(s). Lottery winners use trusts to protect their jackpot and ensure professional management of their winnings. A trust is basically a deed which outlines who owns or gets ownership of what, and when, how, and where that will happen. Think of a trust as a huge pot of gold created to safely place assets inside of. A person sets up a trust and figures out what property, cash or assets they want to place inside of the trust. It could be money, real estate, valuable art, family heirlooms, stock or other assets.

There are three major parties to a trust: the grantor, the trustee and the beneficiary. A lottery winner who sets up a trust is known as the Grantor or Settlor. The Grantor chooses a person to oversee and manage the trust, known as the Trustee or Administrator. This person oversees investment of assets in the trust, tax returns and making sure the beneficiaries receive payments from the trust. A trust can be set up for the benefit of one or more Beneficiaries. A grantor of a trust can also be the trustee and the beneficiary of that same trust.

The laws for structuring a trust are state-specific, so it's imperative that you consult with a practicing attorney who can explain your legal options to you. A revocable trust means the Grantor, or person responsible for setting up the trust, has the power to revoke, change the terms of, or end the trust and take back any assets that remain inside of the trust. If the grantor dies, the revocable trust then becomes an irrevocable trust and can no longer be revoked or modified. In an irrevocable trust the grantor has relinquished all control over the property and cannot change the provisions of a trust.

There are many different types of trusts. The attorney will draw up the trust and you can appoint a Trustee to manage the assets and make payments on your behalf. You'll have the option to set up separate trusts for your children, trusts that benefit the family and trusts that serve charitable giving. Some of the options available for a lottery winner to claim the prize might be: general or limited partnerships, revocable and/or irrevocable trusts and blind trusts. The option chosen by the lottery winner to receive the payout (cash or annuity) impacts the ability to fund a trust or entity.

Remember, a winning lottery ticket is kind of like a blank, signed check. It is a bearer instrument and can be made out to whomever signs the ticket. Most winners rush to sign the ticket right away and keep it safe until they can redeem it at the lottery commission headquarters. Unfortunately, with most states publicizing the names of lottery winners, their lives can become a living hell overnight. A blind trust is a type of trust that allows lottery winners to keep their names private and lets the trust claim the winnings instead.

A grantor sets up a blind trust, naming himself as beneficiary and naming a third party as trustee. The third party trustees may be the winner's attorneys and/or financial advisors. The grantor funds the trust by donating the winning lottery ticket into the trust before the prize is claimed. The trustee signs the lottery ticket and the trust now owns the lottery ticket, transferring the asset to the trust. The trustees can now step forward to claim the prize money in the name of the trust, allowing the grantor/beneficiary to remain anonymous if their state allows. The trustee has full authority over how the assets in the trust are invested and the grantor has no knowledge of how the trustee invests the assets, hence "blind." A blind trust keeps the names of lottery winners off the record books, however it is irrevocable, so backing out of it should you change your mind later could prove to be very difficult, if not impossible.

If tickets were purchased as part of a group forming a trust, a legal partnership, or some type of entity to collect the winnings might be an option. The lottery rules for some states dictate that there can only be one person receiving the payout per winning lottery ticket. If a group forms some sort of entity this will allow them all to claim the prize, as opposed to just one person representing the group. If one person claims the prize and distributes shares to other members of the group, those shares may be considered gifts by the IRS and therefore subject to gift tax.

Coming into wealth suddenly will undoubtedly present new challenges to consider. Consult with an estate-planning attorney to address issues such as estate tax in the event of your death, and how you will transfer assets. For example, a lottery winner chooses to receive annual payments over 25 years and dies during the 5th year of pay-outs. The decedent's estate has to be tallied up and taxes have to be assessed. The remaining annuity payments for the next 20 years are counted as part of the lottery winner's gross estate, even though the family has not yet received the payments. The significance of this is that taxes are assessed against those future annuity payments and the family may not have enough money available to pay the federal and state tax due on the estate.

It could take the family years to pay off that tax bill, unless they had an irrevocable life insurance trust (ILIT). An ILIT is a trust funded with a life insurance policy on the life of the lottery winner. If something were to happen to the winner, his/her beneficiaries could receive the proceeds from the trust and settle any tax bills. Consult with an estate planning attorney to design the most tax-advantageous trusts to receive payments and minimize taxes.

An estate planning attorney can help you address concerns about when and if, you are going to allow your children to inherit money and the best vehicle to transfer wealth to your dependents. Minor children need guardians appointed and an estate-planning attorney can help you make that decision about who would be best to help raise your children should you and/or your spouse pass away. You may have previously appointed someone to be the godmother or godfather of your children many years ago in a church ceremony, but is that really the person best-suited to raise your children now that circumstances have changed? What provisions have you made for your children in the event that you or your spouse dies? Surely, there are plenty of folks that would want to take care of the children of a suddenly wealthy family member, but who would be the person best suited for the job? How much money will you allow your children's guardians to access to meet the expenses of raising your children? When will you turn the rest of the money over to your children to control? Will you let them inherit all of the money at once, or will you give the money to them in increments? Perhaps you could have it disbursed to give them some when they turn 21, more at age 28 and the final installments at age 35?

An estate planning attorney can help you draft living trusts, prenuptial agreements, wills, power-of-attorney, and advance medical directives. This attorney can also calculate estate or inheritance taxes, and can refer you to competent life insurance agents that are licensed and certified by the state to sell life insurance products.

It's a good idea to do some estate planning even if you never win the lottery or don't have a sizeable estate. Today, everything is done electronically. Have you considered how your family would access your information if something were to happen to you? Consider assembling an estate planning notebook and storing the following information inside of it:

- A copy of your will, along with the location of the original will and who has authorized access to it.
- List of the location of all of your assets: trusts, banks, brokerage companies, retirement accounts on the job and privately held.
- List all of the life insurance: policies owned by you, life insurance with your job, life insurance with any other partnership, association or organization.
- List of beneficiary designations for the assets and policies.
- Copies of any Advance Medical Directives, Power of Attorneys
- Location of Birth Certificates, Marriage licenses, Divorce licenses, social security statements, passports, etc.
- Copy any Personal Letter of Instruction, Funeral Contracts
- List of people to be contacted in the event of your death

- Location of the passwords for your online accounts

Chapter 9: Taxes, Death and Trouble...

You will need finance professionals to help you understand the tax implications of your win, help you manage your day-to-day living expenses, and establish and maintain long-term investments. Some of these professionals may function well in multiple areas. Hiring an accountant and/or financial advisor before you collect the winnings is a great idea, as they will help formulate a strategy for you to manage and maximize your money. Financial/Tax Practitioners specialize in different areas of money and can be hired, or paid in different ways. Your tax person may not necessarily be the best person to discuss the growth of your investments with.

Pay attention to the initials behind the names of your financial professionals. All of those letters could look like a can of alphabet soup, but if ever there were a time when those abbreviations mean something, it is now. As it relates to taxes, there are several different specialists you can hire: a Tax Attorney, a Certified Public Accountant (CPA) and/or an Enrolled Agent (EA). All of these tax specialists are licensed and certified to handle tax-related matters, but their expertise, education and level of training could vary. Some of them may specialize in serving corporate entities; others are experienced in arguing cases against the IRS, still others may focus more on serving individual clients and their families. You can expect these professionals to have a level of expertise far above the average tax preparer working at H & R Block during tax season. You'll need a professional that can both prepare and sign tax returns on your behalf and represent you in case of an IRS audit.

The tax piece is a huge consideration for most lottery winners because prize money is taxable to the recipient as *personal ordinary income*. The state sponsoring the lottery withholds federal income tax and may withhold state income tax, depending upon where you live and where you bought the lottery ticket.

At the time of this writing, the following states assess no personal state income tax: Alaska, Florida, New Hampshire, Nevada, South Dakota, Tennessee, Texas, Washington and Wyoming. Seven states do not participate in the lottery at all: Alabama, Alaska, Hawaii, Mississippi, Nevada, Utah and Wyoming. Both Nevada and Alaska assess no personal income tax and sell no lottery tickets, but that doesn't necessarily mean you won't owe tax in the state where you purchased your ticket. States may have special resident and non-resident withholding rates. Both Pennsylvania and California exempt lottery winnings from personal income taxation, although California requires that you buy the winning lottery ticket in the state of California in order for it to be exempt. Delaware used to exempt lottery winnings but they do not anymore and the District of Columbia taxes lottery winnings as well.

The state lottery commission withholds federal and state (if applicable) income tax in the year that you receive the money, but that withholding doesn't mean you won't owe any additional tax. Winners *still* need to file a tax return the following year. Employees who receive wages or a salary may have tax withheld through-out the year from their paychecks, but if their employer did not withhold enough to cover their tax liability they will still owe taxes when they file their tax return. Similarly, the lottery commission may not withhold enough to cover the actual tax due and you can find yourself with a whopping tax bill for the year in which you won. Remember, prize money is taxed as *personal ordinary income*. A good tax professional can help you estimate the taxes that will be due and set aside those monies in a separate account reserved just for taxes.

At the time of this writing, the IRS requires taxes be automatically withheld from any lottery prize over $5,000. If you give the lottery commission your social security number, they are required to withhold 25% of your winnings for federal taxes. If you do not give the lottery commission your social security number they can withhold 28% of your winnings for federal taxes, this is in addition to any state tax that may be applicable. The amount of tax you actually owe will be according to your tax bracket.

Lottery prize winnings are taxed as personal ordinary income. The lottery prize money received gets added to the earnings the winner may have already received from work or their business during that tax year. Alimony, jury duty pay, royalties and other income may be also calculated as personal income, so consult a tax professional. In the United States, personal income tax brackets are progressive. As personal income increases, more tax is assessed. The 2016 tax brackets and rates are:

Rate	Single Filers	Married Filing Joint	Head of Household Filers
10%	$0 to $9,275	$0 to $18,550	$0 to $13,250
15%	$9,275 to $37,650	$18,550 to $75,300	$13,250 to $50,400
25%	$37,650 to $91,150	$75,300 to $151,900	$50,400 to $130,150
28%	$91,150 to $190,150	$151,900 to $231,450	$130,150 to $210,800
33%	$190,150 to $413,350	$231,450 to $413,350	$210,800 to $413,350
35%	$413,350 to $415,050	$413,350 to $466,950	$413,350 to $441,000
39.6%	$415,050+	$466,950+	$441,000+

A recent Powerball lottery had a $1.5 billion jackpot. If just one person won the prize and opted to take the lump sum, the tax piece might look something like this:

- $1.5 billion prize = $930 million lump sum payout
- 39.6% x $930 million = $369 million in federal taxes due (lottery commission automatically takes 25% and the rest will be owed at tax filing time).
- Virginia assesses a 5.75% tax on any income over $17,000 so if I won, I'd owe the Commonwealth $53 million (Lottery commission automatically withholds 4% for the state and I owe the rest at tax time).
- My take home pay would be around $508 million.

This is why you'd want to consult a tax professional and an estate planning attorney right away!

In Chapter 2 we talked about how the time value of money impacts the decision to take the lump sum versus the annuity. The example we gave was as follows:

A jackpot advertised as $100 million is based on the assumption that the person will take $5 million payouts each year, for 20 years. The Lottery Commission will invest a lump sum of about $57,349,500 at 6% interest. This is enough to fund a stream of payments worth $5 million each year for 20 years totaling $100 million. If the winner chooses to take the entire jackpot now, then they only gets what's in the pot now.... the principal, which is $57,349.500. The winner pays federal and state income taxes on that amount and takes home $35 million.

Normally, a lottery winner who gets the option to take the lump sum or receive payments as an annuity **after** they win the lottery must include the *full value* of the prize money in personal income tax calculation immediately, even if he/she takes the annuity over time. The constructive receipt doctrine is a federal rule that says taxpayers are subject to income tax on money they have an unrestricted right to obtain, whether or not the taxpayer actually receives all of the money; but there are exceptions to that rule.

Some lottery games require a ticket purchaser to indicate whether they will receive payouts as a lump sum or an annuity, at the time of sale. If a lottery winner chose the cash option when they bought the ticket, **before** they actually win the lottery, but elects to receive annual payments **after** they discover that they're the winner, the constructive receipt doctrine does not apply and income tax will be due as the lottery winner receives payouts each year.

Another exception to the rule is called the qualified prize option. If your state permits lottery winners to use the qualified prize option, the winner of the lottery has 60 days after winning to decide how to take the money. As long as the lottery winner makes that decision within 60 days after winning, they will not be subject to the constructive receipt doctrine if they elect to take the annuity over at least ten years, and won't have to pay tax on the full amount of the prize immediately. Check with your state lottery commission to determine if it has adopted the qualified prize option. Consulting with a tax professional before collecting your winnings can help you take advantage of other tax strategies.

Professional tax planning can also help facilitate your charitable giving, because it's not as simple as it may seem. Generous lottery winners might want to buy houses and cars for family members and lend them huge sums of money. Many aren't aware that a federal gift tax, and in some cases, a state gift tax applies to all US citizens. Generally speaking, when transferring ownership of property or money, a gift tax is imposed on the giver of the gift unless the recipient falls into the exempt category:

- Gifts made to a U.S. citizen spouse.
- A gift of tuition or medical expenses as long as the donor pays the institution directly.
- Gifts made to a qualified charity by a US citizen
- Gifts that are under the annual exclusion limit for the calendar year.

At the time of this writing (2016) a US citizen can exclude from gift tax the first $14,000 worth of gifts for the year to each recipient. Anything over that amount is subject to gift tax. The gift tax annual exclusion can be doubled to $28,000 for a married US citizen. So a married lottery winner can "split-gift" with their spouse and give their child or someone else up to $28,000 per calendar year without triggering the gift tax. There is a lifetime gift-tax exclusion of $5.45 million (in 2016). A finance professional or estate attorney would be the best person to help you take advantage of tax planning strategies to maximize these exemptions and credits.

When giving money to charities you need to consider their business structure and if they are a public charity, or a private foundation. If they are a non-profit 501c3 organization then your gift may be tax deductible, which would be to your advantage, as opposed to giving gifts to a charity with no formal structure. You can insist that recipients sign confidentiality agreements as a condition of accepting your gift, if that is important to you.

Due to the complexity of giving at this level, you will need to discuss the best ways to support charitable giving with your tax professional or attorney. There are options to create your own private charitable foundation, or make direct contributions to various charities or use a donor-advised fund to facilitate your giving. Lottery winners are inundated with requests for donations. Designate a firm family member, or a member of your financial team to weed through and turn down the numerous requests for money. When people ask you for cash you can respond with, "My money guy handles that," and refer all of the requests over to this person. This person can carefully consider requests and send a firm "thanks but no thanks" to most people and refer requests that should receive further consideration to you personally.

Whether you opted to take your lottery winnings as annual payments or a lump sum, your finance professional can show you strategies for charitable giving throughout the year that will minimize your tax liabilities. As your investments grow you will incur taxes on those gains. Capital gains on investments are taxed differently than ordinary earned income. Your finance professional can help you calculate the net or after-tax return on various investments you may be considering, as well as identify and recommend tax-deferred investments, tax-exempt income, and tax-exempt investments that are appropriate for your situation.

An accountant receives payment at an hourly rate, or a fixed fee. They inspect and audit financial records for individuals or companies. Accountants may also prepare tax returns, tax planning and to a certain degree, financial planning.

Accountants must pass a state exam before being issued a license to practice as a Certified Public Accountant (CPA), and are bound by ethical standards of behavior in that state.

- To find a Certified Public Account, contact the American Institute of CPAs (AICPA): http://www.aicpa.org/FORTHEPUBLIC/FINDACPA/Pages/FindACPA.aspx

- To verify the credentials of a CPA by state, go to: http://www.aicpa.org/Advocacy/State/StateContactInfo/Pages/StateContactInformation.aspx

An enrolled agent has the highest credentials the Internal Revenue Service awards. They are federally licensed and have unlimited rights to represent taxpayers before the IRS. They've either passed a three-part comprehensive IRS test covering individual and business tax returns, or they gained their experience as a former IRS employee. Enrolled Agents must adhere to ethical standards and complete 72 hours of continuing education courses every three years.

- Contact the National Association of Enrolled Agents to Find an EA: http://www.naea.org/taxpayers/what-enrolled-agent

Chapter 10: Money, Money, Money.... Can You Handle It?

Financial Advisors/Planners can help you make wise decisions with your newfound wealth but they are not all created equally. Just because someone works as a stockbroker on Wall Street, it doesn't mean they know the best investment strategies to maximize your windfall. Titles, designations and certifications mean varying levels of education, experience and training. Knowing how to find and vet a financial advisor can help you determine who belongs on your finance team and in what capacity.

Anyone can hang their shingle out and call themselves a Financial Advisor. Unlike being a medical doctor, nurse, or licensed cosmetologist, you don't necessarily have to have any specific licensing or certification to advise folks about their money. People throw around titles like Senior Financial Planner or Expert Wealth & Assets Manager and while they may seem trustworthy, not everyone is qualified to serve you. Some folks may seem to know a lot about managing money and may even seem to have your best interests in mind, yet they have no formal training or education to be in the financial planning/advice business. These are **exactly** the types you'll want to avoid.

Personal finance is not a subject most people learn about in school. We learn how to manage money, for better or for worse, from our parents and significant others throughout our lives. It might not be a bad idea to work with someone that can teach the basics of managing money, budgeting, debt management, credit, risk management, investment, and estate planning, before you ever win a dime on a lottery ticket. Someone who neither sells investments products, nor makes a commission off of their recommendations would be ideal to work with before you come into your fortune. This type of financial educator can put you in a better position to ask really great questions of the financial advisors you will eventually hire to manage your money. Financial counselors may charge by the hour and offer services in person or virtually. A recent lottery winner might consider hiring financial counselors and financial coaches to educate not only themselves, but their family members as well, since they too will be impacted by the lottery win.

Financial Educators can be found with the following titles: Accredited Financial Counselor® (AFC®), Financial Coaches, Financial Consultants, or Budget and Credit Counselors. Check to see what credentialing body certifies the person before working with them. Some are primarily financial educators teaching people how to understand money or financial literacy (this is the category I am currently in). Others offer advice on handling money, but may also sell various financial products. Watch out for "educational seminars" and "investment dinners" which are sometimes no more than sales pitches to get you to buy certain financial products.

A financial educator may be the ideal person to help you navigate the basics of money and money management. Financial educators typically do not sell investment products or securities (though they may be licensed to do so). A recent lottery winner should make learning about money their new full time job. Increasing your fiscal literary is one of the most important things you can do to preserve your newfound wealth.

Before you claim your lottery winnings, you will need a competent Financial Advisor on your team. It's important that you stick with professional designations that can be vetted by a national professional certification body. A CERTIFIED FINANCIAL PLANNER® (CFP®), Certified Public Accountant (CPA®), Chartered Financial Consultant (ChFC®), Chartered Life Underwriter (CLU®) and Registered Investment Advisor (RIA®) are some of the more popular credentials. Those who hold these credentials have extensive education and experience and have passed mandatory testing standards to hold these credentials.

Financial Professionals who hold the certifications above are able to thoroughly assess your financial position and make specific recommendations about managing your money based on the information you provide them with. They will provide you with a broad financial plan that may include recommendations for debt management, investments, education planning, retirement planning, insurance and estate planning. Some financial planners don't execute the plans on your behalf or sell any financial products to you. These types of planners work on a "fee-only" basis, which means they don't stand to make any commission off of the financial products they are recommending to you. They charge an hourly rate for their services.

Other financial advisors make a comprehensive plan for you, but they also sell financial products and may earn a commission on the products they sell. They invest your money on your behalf and earn a percentage of all that they manage for you. These planners are "fee-based". Ask your planner to explain how they will be compensated. Does the planner stand to benefit by getting a commission off of anything they recommend? All of this should be outlined in the terms of agreement you sign before you ever begin working with them. Consider limiting yourselves only to advisors that will list these details in writing.

Ask the potential financial advisor what their title or certification means, and what kind of education, licensing and/or experience was required to get it. Find the organization that awards the advisor their designation or accreditation. Many professional certifications require a practitioner to maintain a certain amount of continued education units (CEU's) in order to maintain their certification. This ensures that the practitioner keeps learning after they get certified - which contributes to their knowledge base. Ask how they maintain their designation/credential and check to verify their status. The certification/credentialing body they fall under should have a process to check the status of their license and to see if they've ever been disciplined for unethical behavior. Before you work with someone, find out where you can file a complaint if you have a problem with the financial advisor.

It's a good idea to work with a financial advisor experienced in managing high net-worth clients. Some advisors will *only* work with individuals who have 7 or 8 figure net-worth and carry no consumer related debt (i.e. credit cards). Others will only take on clients that allow them to manage assets in excess of a certain dollar amount. A lottery winner who takes home a $300 million jackpot should work with a financial advisor used to handling that level of cash, rather than leaving it in the hands of someone who has only managed portfolios worth $1 million in assets.

All financial advisors licensed to sell investment and insurance products are essentially brokers. While some brokers are also advisors, other brokers function primarily as salespeople and **all** they do is sell product. They may work for a brokerage firm, a financial planning firm or a bank and have titles like: stockbrokers, investment representatives, or registered representatives. They have passed specific state exams to obtain a broker's license. Series 6, Series 7, Series, 63, Series 65, and Series 66 are some of the more popular licenses they may hold. The broker's license allows them to sell financial products such as stocks, bonds and insurance in the state in which they are licensed. They must be registered with the Financial Industry Regulatory Authority (FINRA), and the brokerage firm they work for must be registered with the US government's Security Exchange Commission (SEC).

FINRA is responsible for regulating member brokerage firms. FINRA also has authority to regulate the exchange markets. The government agency with ultimate oversight over FINRA and the entire securities industry is The Securities Exchange Commission (SEC). Both agencies have portals that allow you to check the status of a broker, financial advisor, or insurance salesperson. FINRA provides a free Broker Check site to check compliance records. Just type in the name of the financial advisor you are considering to confirm licensure, certifications, and whether there are any ethical or legal concerns reported. You can see how long the person has held licenses in the investments community and if they are current. It's all there. Carefully vet each advisor before discussing your situation. Make sure they are not connected with any scams, frauds, lawsuits, suspensions etc.

Part of the reason why you want a financial advisor that has verifiable credentials is that they may be held to specific standards as it relates to advising you about your money. Some financial advisors are held to the highest level of fiduciary standards in the industry. This ensures that their interests aren't opposed to your own; and they are bound by the responsibility to make decisions that are in your best interest as their client. Financial advisors bound by a fiduciary standard may have the following designations: Registered Investment Advisors (RIA®) or Investment Advisor Representative (IAR®). A CERTIFIED FINANCIAL PLANNER® (CFP®) is held to a fiduciary standard, regardless of whether they are fee-only or fee-based. They cannot sell you a product that is not a good plan for you simply because they stand to make a commission from it.

Your financial advisor is going to be one of the most important folks on your team. Ideally, you can have a long and prosperous relationship with one advisor or with one firm that specializes in wealthy families. There are many different financial concerns you'll need to address with your advisor. Let's examine some of the topics that might come up should you suddenly find yourself with a ton of money.

You'll need to decide how to claim your prize and your financial advisor can crunch the numbers with you and help you decide if it's best for you to take the lump sum, or to take the money in annual installments payable over 29 years. Depending upon your level of money management or how closely you work with your advisors, it may be better to do one versus the other. Annual payments may help someone who has a tendency to make poor financial decisions. Collecting the payments each year might give a person time to learn how to manage the windfall and make better financial decisions rather than running through all of the money at once.

Once folks know you have money, they may start to treat you like the "Bank of Zamunda," asking you for gifts, loans to start businesses, or for your participation in their investments and/or "get rich quick" schemes. Use your financial team as a barrier between you and all the people who want to get next to your money. Find the toughest, most no-nonsense person on your team and reroute all requests for money through that person. Ensure they know what financial goals are closely aligned with yours, and empower them to sift through these sorts of requests. Your financial team can help you decide which causes to give to and which ones to pass by.

Do not invest in anything you do not understand! You will need to decide which projects you're going to invest in and why. Invest the bulk of your winnings so that you can live comfortably off of the interest and never run out of money. For the most part, you'll invest in ventures that will earn income - products where you don't even have to touch the principal; just let the interest compound. It's recommended that you put most of your money in investments and not even touch it for six months after you win. Use this time to get used to having money, paying off current debts and learning all you can about how to make good decisions with the money.

In addition to preserving the bulk of your winnings and positioning your money to last for your lifetime and beyond, you'll need help to plan your day-to-day living expenses and general spending. Let your financial advisor put you on a budget for the things you intend to splurge on. I read about a family that won $350 million dollars in the lottery and their financial advisors put the family on a $300,000 per month spending budget. After a few months of this, the family figured out that they didn't even need that much money to live on and reduced their spending budget down to $100,000 per month.

Short term spending may include a couple of splurges. Winning a lot of money in the lottery might allow you to indulge a bit. Now's the time to consider the things you've always wanted to have. What are the things on your "wish-list"? Do you value experiences over things? If so, what's on your bucket-list? What are some of the things that make you smile? Are you happy watching others be happy? If so, what are the limitations (if any) on your giving? Your financial planner will help you identify the implications of some of your purchases.

Most people say that the first thing they'll do when they win the lottery is buy a big house and pay cash for it. I've heard of lottery winners who purchased a big house for cash and never considered the ongoing property tax and insurance obligations. Unfortunately, they had to sell those large houses because they couldn't meet the tax obligations after the bulk of their jackpot was spent. A financial planner can help you plan to meet financial obligations five, ten or even thirty years down the line.

A wise financial planner can help you explore alternatives you might not have previously considered in order to make the most cost-efficient decisions. Is there an option to *rent* the home of your dreams temporarily rather than outright *buying* it? This would give you time to experience just how much the electric bill on a 10,000 square-foot home is, and time to explore other expenses connected with owning a large property. You'll figure out if you need to hire household staff like: a butler, maid, groundskeepers, maintenance professionals, and/or a nanny to help manage the property and serve your family. Your financial planner can help you crunch the numbers to determine how to pay your household staff's salaries, taxes, and other benefits. While renting a home temporarily, you might even discover that your new lifestyle doesn't keep you in the same city long enough to even enjoy living in that 10,000 square-foot new home.

Many people express the desire to buy animals if ever they won the lottery. Figure out the cost of land to build stables to board the horse(s), salaries for the people who will tend to your animals, along with the food budget and veterinary care for the animals. If you're considering buying a plane, your advisor will help you consider the financial implications of that decision. How much will it cost to acquire land and build a hangar or will you keep your private jet parked somewhere other than home? Who do you hire to fly the plane, and who will maintain the plane, keep gas in it, and how much does all that cost? If you buy a fleet of cars where do you garage them? How do you plan to insure these vehicles, as well as provide fuel and maintenance costs? Your financial planner will help you consider the additional expenses connected to every purchase you could possibly make.

Another thing most potential lottery winners say they will do is quit their day job. You'll need to decide if you're going to quit your job right away, in the near future, or perhaps switch gears and work on other things you've always wanted to do. For some folks quitting their job is a no-brainer; but others may need a financial advisor to help them determine the best time to resign their current position. It may not be an option for you to work at the same job or around the same people after you win. Perhaps your supervisor may fear that you no longer have the incentive to take direction, or your co-workers may become jealous of your newfound wealth.

A financial advisor can help you determine the best way to finance a business you've always wanted to run. You might be able to work for yourself, or work in another capacity that will continue to allow you to earn money and express your talents, skills and abilities. Winning the lottery may afford you the chance to explore a career that you've always wanted to pursue, but didn't because you lacked the funds to go back to school and get a degree or necessary certificate. Financial freedom puts you in the position where you no longer *need* to go out and earn a living, but perhaps you *want* to take classes simply for your own enjoyment.

You'll need someone to help you handle insurance-related matters. Your estate-planning attorney or financial advisor should be able to connect you with someone to purchase life insurance, medical insurance, property insurance for your estate and any motor vehicles you may purchase (including an airplane). You'll also need to be adequately insured in various business endeavors and may have to insure the lives or offer medical insurance on behalf of any employees. The state licensed insurance agent can help you weigh the benefits of self-insurance versus purchasing insurance policies. They'll help you explore the differences between term insurance versus whole life insurance, variable annuities and universal life insurance policies. They can also explain any tax-advantages afforded to you by the purchase of any of these products, as well as the investment component of such policies.

- Check your State Insurance Regulator to find a state licensed insurance agent - http://www.naic.org/state_web_map.htm

I spoke with Ms. Paula Pass, President and CEO of Arkagos Advisors + Asset Management in Alexandria, Virginia. Her firm has built a reputation for delivering straightforward financial advice instead of selling investment products. They provide thoughtful, transparent and goal-oriented financial planning and asset management that puts the client's needs first. Paula shared valuable tips to keep in mind when selecting an agent/advisor to purchase life insurance from.

Paula begins with making sure clients understand that insurance is a product that is purchased to defer some type of risk – verses an investment. Risk management is a form of wealth management or wealth preservation. You should insure those things that would be difficult to replace should they be lost. A client with sudden wealth contacting Paula's firm and seeking management and advice could expect the following process:

- Understanding of the client, their back ground, history with money, debt, spending habits, future goals and dreams.
- Design of a plan to protect the principal and generate investment returns that are in line with the client's risk profile, in addition to being tax efficient.
- Estate planning for future generations and protection of legacy.
- In protecting the principal assets and managing overall risk, Paula's firm defines insurance needs first, investment strategies second and a plan for needed cash flow of projected returns in a most tax-efficient manner.

A person who comes into sudden wealth and finds themselves to be the winner of $300 million after taxes would need to consider a variety of insurance products, based on their goals and objectives. Paula's firm encourages clients that are generally more philanthropic-oriented to use various insurance products and annuities as instruments to manage the funding of a charitable lead or grantor trust as a first recommendation. She also recommends an umbrella policy, as statistically, people with large sums of money tend to get sued.

Paula encourages anyone seeking to purchase life insurance to contact the State Insurance Commissioner to see if there have been any complaints registered with the agent from which they intend to purchase. Secondly, find out how many companies with which the agent has appointments. The more companies that the agent is associated with, the greater the access that agent has to find the appropriate policy to meet the client's needs without being backed into a corner to only offer one line of product. Having access to multiple carriers reduces the conflict of interest and provides a greater service to the client. Lastly, find out if the agent is fully licensed, not just for insurance; but also licensed as a broker and a fiduciary.

When choosing and vetting a person selling life insurance, the types of credentials they should have depends on the type of insurance product being purchased. FINRA has oversight with variable annuities, as the internal investment choices are generally mutual funds or Exchange-Traded Funds, which require a Series 7 license in order to transact. So in addition to a state health and life license, the investment professional should also have the Series 7 license in order to sell variable annuities.

There are Fixed Indexed Annuities and Fixed Annuities that fall under the oversight of the State Insurance Commissioner, and they have quite a bit a power as it relates to oversight. In order to sell the latter two products and any other life insurance products, a person would need a life and health license in the state that the agent resides. They would also need to have an established business along with a valid non-resident license in the state where the client has their legal residence (if different than the agent's state of legal residence). No other FINRA license or registration is required to sell these type of annuities. Life Insurance and annuities are separate products sometimes sold by the same company.

Life insurance, regardless of whole life, variable or universal, provides tax deferred growth. If set up correctly, it can provide a death benefit or in some cases, a stream of tax-free income through a borrowing strategy. Purchasing a life insurance policy to replace the potential earnings of the insured is not a main goal for people who have received a windfall, as their ability to "earn" money is not the focus. Protecting their money through safe, tax-deferred growth is the main objective. Annuities can also provide tax-deferred growth. Taking those assets out have different tax consequences.

Basically, all insurance products offer tax-deferred growth without regard to income limits.

The benefit of a life insurance policy payout after death, if taken as a lump sum, is tax free without limit for individuals. Annuities provide tax-deferred growth and are targeted at creating income that cannot be outlived. Some life insurance policies can be structured to provide tax -free income that the client can "borrow" from the policy and drawdown on the principal.

For lottery winners that may have previously lived from paycheck to paycheck, their ability to appropriately vet tax advisors, CPA's or any financial professional might be limited initially. The best approach in this case, is to work with a financial professional that has the ability to use CDAR's or short-term brokered CD's to keep the money safe within FDIC limits. This will buy them enough time to research and retain the appropriate individual to go forward in creating a long term financial plan and strategy.

Essentially, the financial professional will be directing and managing their assets. They will also be responsible for educating that person about the power of the "future value" of money, and developing patterns of financial discipline through "financial therapy". Most financial advisors stay away from making blanket financial statements; however, it is a general rule that anyone who has received a windfall of money needs to take things *very* slowly. A great deal of estate planning should be done first, as that will provide the advisor the ground work for developing a personal investment policy statement. This is literally a written document describing the investing "rules" for that person and their family, inclusive of insurance needs.

Ms. Paula Pass also addressed the concept of 'The Family Business' or Family Practice as it relates to managing high net-worth individuals, which is essentially a private practice financial planning firm that serves only a few very high net-worth clients. The services are broad and comprehensive; inclusive of asset management, insurance, estate planning and tax planning. The main purpose of using the services of a Family Practice is to provide broad and inclusive attention to all aspects of the client's portfolio. Even a very slight change in any one of the previously mentioned items in the client's portfolio can create an opportunity for potential growth, or an equal opportunity to use a protection strategy to avert large scale losses. Managing a portfolio of $300M is equal to managing an institutional fund and requires active supervision to keep the assets balanced, protected and on track with meeting the clients short and long-term objectives.

Ms. Paula Pass's website offers a wealth of information about the services her firm offers: http://www.arkagosadvisors.com

Private Banks may use wealth management divisions for suitable investment options. Check the credential of the person who works at the banks you patronize. Check the licensing and status of your banker, bank trust officer, and investment banker before you give them massive business. Consider interviewing at least 3 different planners before selecting one. Use the following resources to check the backgrounds of various financial professionals:

Certified Financial Planner Board of Standards, Inc. (CFP®)

1425 K. St. NW, Suite 500
Washington, DC 20005
1-888-487-1497
www.cfp.net

The Certified Financial Planner Board of Standards is a regulatory organization that fosters professional standards in personal financial Planning. The CFP Board works to ensure that the public benefits from competent financial planning. The CFP Board certifies Financial Planners who meet its requirements by granting use of its trademarks.

Financial Planning Association (FPA)
4100 E. Mississippi Ave., Suite 400
Denver, CO 80246
1-800-322-4237
www.fpanet.org

The FPA is a leadership and advocacy organization connecting those who provide services with the consumers they serve. This organization is a resource for the public to find educational resources and financial planners to offer advice using an ethical, objective, client-centered process.

The National Association of Personal Financial Advisors
8700 W. Bryn Mawr Avenue, Suite 700N
Chicago, IL 60631
1-888-FEE-ONLY (888-333-6659
www.napfa.org

NAPFA is the country's leading professional association of Fee-Only financial advisor – highly trained professionals who are committed to working in the best interests of those they serve. NAPFA financial professionals meet the highest membership standards, never earn a commission and have no incentive to sell you one product over another.

The Financial Industry Regulatory Authority
(FINRA)
1736 K St., NW
Washington, DC 20006
1-800-289-9999
www.finra.org
FINRA Broker Check –
http://brokercheck.finra.org/
FINRA professional designations and organizations locator –
https://www.finra.org/investors/professional-designations

FINRA is the largest independent regulator for all securities firms doing business in the United States. The organization operates the largest dispute resolution forum in the securities industry for disputes between investors and securities firms.

Garrett Planning Network, Inc.
103 E. Van Buren, #140
Eureka Springs, AR 72632
913-268-1500

www.garrettplanning.com

The Garrett Planning Network has a nationwide membership with hundreds of independent, Fee-Only Financial Planners providing advice to people from all walks of life, without minimum account requirements, sales commissions, or long-term commitments. Members proudly embrace their fiduciary duty, always placing their clients' best interest first.

Securities and Exchange Commission Headquarters
100 F Street, NE
Washington, DC 20549
202-942-8088

The Securities and Exchange Commission (SEC) is a federal agency responsible for protecting investors, maintaining fair and efficient markets, and facilitating capital formation. The SEC has broad authority over investment markets and organizations which offer investments to the public. They enforce securities laws and can bring civil actions against individuals and companies for violation of these laws. The Central Registration Depository (CDR) is a computerized database containing information about most brokers, their representatives, and the firms they work for. You can find out if brokers are properly licensed in your state and if they have had disciplinary problems with regulators or received serious complaints from investors. You can also find information about the brokers' educational backgrounds and where they've worked before their current jobs.

- SEC Investment Advisor Public Disclosure Database – http://www.adviserinfo.sec.gov/IAPD/Default.aspx

State securities regulators enforce state securities laws. They license securities firms and investment professionals, register certain securities offerings, review financial offerings of small companies and audit securities firm branch offices.

- Check your state securities regulator – http://www.nasaa.org/about-us/contact-us/contact-your-regulator/

Chapter 11: Money 101

If reading about all of this has been exhausting, how much more do you think it would be to actually win the lottery and have to consider all of this in real-life and real-time? Ultimately, winning the lottery is a problem most people *wish* they had the opportunity to solve. Take financial classes to learn more about managing money. As a new lottery winner, learning how to manage money should become your new full-time job. Why not start now? There are plenty of classes available on personal finance. I'm going to review some basic pointers that may be helpful to consider right here, right now, wherever you are financially- *before* you come into a boat-load of money.

The number one reason lottery winners' blow through their jackpots is the lack of financial education and being ill prepared to manage sudden wealth. Building on these principles now might put you in a better position later to preserve and grow your lottery winnings. It will also benefit you whether you're currently managing a five, six or seven-figure salary or living paycheck to paycheck. These tips may be helpful to know … *period.*

Before you invest a red nickel or a thin dime, it's crucial to understand why you want to invest. While the logical answer (once you've won the lottery) may be, "Because I just won a ton of money and don't want to run through it all and be broke again," you will need to be more specific than that. Starting from right here, right where you are now, define some of the things you want to do with money. What's the timeframe for those goals?

When will you need to have the money to do those things?

Managing your money means figuring out your financial goals and the best way to achieve them. Your financial advisor will help you plan in-depth, but it's a good idea to already have some ideas about what you want to do with your money. Short-term financial goals are things you could accomplish in about a year; mid-term financial goals may take 3-5 years to complete, and long-term financial goals may take up to 10 years or more to complete. The length of time it takes to reach financial goals informs you on the type of investments you should own.

Let's take a look at some basic financial management. Have you budgeted for day-to-day living expenses? Do you have an emergency reserve fund equal to 3-6 months of living expenses? Add up all of your monthly expenses… mortgage, gas, lights, car notes, credit cards, groceries, hobbies and pets. Multiply that figure by 3 or 6, and put that money in a liquid account that you could easily get to in case of an emergency. It's a good idea to have at least 3 months of reserve income if you're a married couple with 2 incomes, and 6 months if you're single or married with only one income.

Eliminate credit card debt. That should be a goal before you have a windfall and one of the first things you want to do, if ever you win some unexpected money…. get rid of consumer debt. Paying 20% interest on a credit card is going to negate any money you earn on your investments.

Make sure you're practicing risk management **now**. This means carrying adequate insurance on the things you can't afford to lose… the things that would be difficult to replace if you ever lost them…. things like your life, your home and your car. Be sure to purchase adequate medical insurance, homeowners or renter's insurance, car insurance, and life insurance.

Calculate your net worth and assess where you are right now. Add up everything you own (your assets) and everything you owe (your liabilities). Subtract your liabilities from your assets to calculate your net worth. Think of your net worth as an Instagram of your financial position. This number is dynamic, like your weight and your credit score. It moves in accordance with the actions you take or fail to take. Constantly monitor your net worth so when you win a ton of money in the lottery, you're not talking about paying off everyone else's bills and buying them houses without having first assessed your own financial position.

- http://www.bankrate.com/calculators/smart-spending/personal-net-worth-calculator.aspx

Understand the difference between investment and savings. Savings is putting your money in the bank and conserving or preserving it, but it doesn't make your money grow. How much is the interest rate you're getting on your average savings/checking account? Like .000000000005 percent… right? The reason why you're getting such a low interest rate on the money is that there is almost no risk involved in saving your money at the bank. Because there's minimal risk, you only earn a low rate of return (interest) on basic checking or savings accounts.

If the bank goes out of business or blows up, most checking accounts, savings accounts, certificate of deposits and Individual Retirement Accounts (IRA) are insured for up to $250,000.00 by the Federal Deposit Insurance Corporation (FDIC). A credit union is a non-profit cooperative type of financial institution owned and run by its members. Most credit union accounts are insured by the National Credit Union Share Insurance Fund (NCUSIF) for up to $250,000 depending upon the type of account.

Banks offer money-market deposit accounts in addition to your more conventional checking account or savings accounts. A MMDA is a type of savings account that provides a higher interest rate in exchange for the higher minimum balance that is usually required. An MMDA may limit check-writing and withdrawal privileges.

A certificate-of-deposit is another bank-insured option that could offer a higher interest rate than your average savings or checking account. You allow the bank to hold your deposit for a certain length of time (3 months, 1-year, 5 years) and a bank issues a certificate equal to your deposit. Generally speaking, the longer the time period, the higher the interest rate. There are usually penalties for withdrawing the money earlier than the specified time. The FDIC and/or NCUA insure these types of bank products.

There is a way you could deposit amounts above the FDIC insured limit into a bank and still be covered. The Certificate of Deposit Account Registry Service (CDARs) is a way to access FDIC Insurance on multimillion-dollar CD deposits and earn interest rates comparable to treasuries and money market mutual funds (which have some degree of risk). CDARs allow you the convenience of working with just *one* member bank within the CDAR network. Let's say you had $1 million dollars to invest. You could deposit the funds with that one network member and the funds would be divided into amounts below the FDIC insurance maximum of $250,000. These smaller amounts are placed with other FDIC-insured CDAR network members. You'd get one statement from your bank detailing the amount of interest earned on *all* of the accounts and other important information. Your confidential information remains protected.

All investment implies risk. The risk is that your investment will grow, but there's also the risk that you could lose it all. Investors take on that risk of gain or loss, in exchange for a higher rate of return on their investments. Return is the amount of money you expect your investment to make over time. The greater the risk, the higher the rate of return you can expect.

Let's go back to those short- mid-, and long-term goals. Your financial goals inform your time frame. Your time horizon informs the types of investments you might find yourself in. Remember we talked about having your emergency savings in a liquid account? Well having it in that bank account earning .00025% means it's not making a whole lot of money in interest, but there are few, if any risks associated with keeping it there. It's liquid because you can easily access those accounts and take the cash out if necessary.

Some of the things that impact risk are time, inflation, and where the country is in the economic cycle. Are we in a recession, depression or are things turning around and making a comeback? The level of volatility in the stock market also impacts risk. Are we in a bear market or a bull market? Things that impact our rate of return are transactions costs, commissions, and taxes. Ideally, we want to invest to at least earn a rate of return higher than inflation.

In Chapter Two we talked about compound interest, which is purely magical... it's when your money makes money. You invest the principal and the principal earns interest. Then, your interest starts to earn interest. For a simple way to estimate compound interest, lets' look at something Albert Einstein invented called "the Rule of 72". If you're considering an investment, take the number 72 and divide it by the annual interest rate of the investment. The answer tells you how long it would take for your principal to double.

For example:

- Invest $1,000 at a 4% interest rate and it would take 18 years for that $1,000 to double to $2,000.
- Invest that same $1,000 at 6%, it would take just 12 years to double.
- Invest the $1,000 at 8%, it would only take 9 years to double.

- Invest the $1,000 at 12% interest and it takes just 6 years to double.

While that may not seem like a whole lot of money, let's use the rule of 72 on a larger amount of money like $256,000. If you invest the principal at 12%, that money doubles to $512,000 in just 6 years. $512,000 becomes $1.2 million in another 6 years. Did I hear you say you don't have 12 years to wait for your money to double? Well… what's your net-worth today and what was your net-worth 12 years ago? Now do you see why you would want to invest your lottery winnings rather than running through it all?

Depending upon the size of your jackpot, your financial planner could place your money in investments designed to earn a higher rate of return. You could have a really good life, just by living off of the interest of your investments. Something else to think about - income from your investments is taxed much lower than personal earned income. Spend and invest wisely with the goal of investing in things that will make you money so that it never runs out.

Risk tolerance is the amount of risk your heart, mind and soul can take while investing and still be able to sleep peacefully at night. It's important that you figure out what your risk tolerance is to be able to understand what type of investments you should be in and/or what your financial advisor has you in. The three basic levels of risk tolerance are: conservative, moderate, or aggressive. Conservative investors are primarily interested in preserving their principal. They're willing to take lower interest rates for slower growth because overall they want to keep their money safe. Moderate investors seek balance in the portfolio. Aggressive investors are willing to take on more risk in exchange for higher rates of return.

- Go to bankrate.com and take the free risk tolerance quiz: http://www.bankrate.com/finance/investing/risk-tolerance-quiz.aspx

Investors classify money in **three main asset classes: cash, bonds and stock**.

Cash – When folks say they have their money in "cash" they are usually referring to bank products that are easily accessible if needed.... easily made "liquid". You'll remember that most bank products are federally insured, so the depositor is not taking on any risk. Because you're not taking on risk with these accounts, depositors don't earn much interest in return.

Bonds – When people say they have their money in "bonds or fixed-income" it means they have loaned money to a municipal agency or corporation in exchange for the return of that principal plus interest payments. Bonds purchased from the federal government, state and municipal bonds, corporate bonds and bond mutual funds invest in corporate or government debt obligations.

People like these kind of investments because of their favorable tax advantage. Also the regular stream of payments received on the bonds can be thought of as income. Bonds generally pay higher rates of return than "cash". There is a direct relationship between the price of a bond and the prevailing interest rates.

When considering bonds, decide on credit quality. Just as you have a personal credit score which determines how much of a risk you are to a lender, bond issuers have a credit rating which indicates how much of a risk their bond is for you to purchase. Consider buying bond mutual funds rather than individual bonds. Bond ratings such as Standard & Poor's, and Moody's indicate the level of risk in investing in a bond. High-grade municipal bonds allow investors to earn tax-exempt income. Discuss the investment alternatives best for you with your financial planner.

Stocks – When folks say they have their money in "stocks or equity" it means they own shares of the company they are invested in. A business will sell a share of ownership (stock) in order to raise money. The capital raised is used to grow the business, buy more machines, hire more people, and conduct more research in order to build a better product and reap higher profits. As a business becomes more profitable, stockholders expect the value of the stock to grow and/or to be paid dividends (a share of the profits). As the company's value rises or falls, so does the value of the stock.

It is important to figure out the different types of stock available and how to read a stock table. There are many online resources available to learn how to evaluate stock, and to practice buying and selling (trading) stock online. A stockbroker has to be licensed to sell investments or securities to you. You can only buy stock through a brokerage house. A full service broker may offer advice on executing trades, retirement planning and tax planning, usually at a high commission. You can find discount brokers online and they usually offer savvy investors ways to buy and sell stock on their own. Brokers should be licensed by the state after having passed Series 6, 7 and/or Series 63 exams.

Stock Market Indexes are an indication of how the market is performing. The S&P 500, Dow Jones Industrial Average, and the NASDAQ are popular benchmarks. Foreign stock indexes like the London, Tokyo, and Toronto exchanges give us an idea of what's happening on a global scale.

Once you know your level of risk tolerance, you'll have an idea of what asset classes you are most comfortable with. Investments can be pictured on a risk pyramid with the more basic investments on the bottom such as your personal family home, cash, and insurance, followed by conservative investments such as US treasury bills and money market mutual funds. Moderate investments such as bond funds and preferred stock are in the middle, with the top of the pyramid consisting of common stock and international stock. The very top of the pyramid is called speculative investments and these are the most aggressive types of investments involving high degrees of risk. They are speculative because you could make a whole lot of money in these types of investments, but you could also lose it all.

It is important to understand market timing. Is it a bear market or a bull market? The way these two animals "attack," gives us an indication of the direction of the financial market. When a bear attacks you, it swipes its claws DOWN, so a bear market means the price of stocks is falling. A bull attacks you by goring you with its horns UP, so a bull market means stocks are rising and folks are showing confidence in investing in the market overall.

Your financial planner will formulate an investment strategy for you based on your stated goals. *Dollar cost averaging* is a commonly used investment strategy. Using regular dollar amount contributions, you buy 'X' amount of investments on a regular periodic basis. When the market goes down your dollars buy more investments than when the market goes up and your dollars buy less investment. Over time it averages out. *Buy-and-Hold* is a common strategy used to build wealth. Wealthy investors tend to hold onto the investments they buy over time. They don't try to time the market, they simply buckle up and sit tight for the long ride.

Diversification reduces the risk of investing by spreading your money among the asset classes. This way you don't put all of your eggs in one basket- all of your money in cash, or all of your investments tied up in the stock market, or all of it in bonds. Asset allocation is making sure you're invested in the right asset classes at the right time. Certain factors determine your asset allocation such as: the amount of time you have to invest, what you intend on using the money for, your current age, assets and other factors. A wise financial planner will keep your money diversified in the right asset classes at the right times.

Mutual funds are groups of stocks, bonds, cash and other investments put together by a mutual funds manager. Investing in a variety of securities allows for instant diversification. The price of a share value of a mutual fund is expressed as NAV – Net Asset Value. There are actively managed mutual funds and passively managed mutual funds. Actively managed funds have fund managers that oversee the mix of stock, bond, cash and other securities in the portfolios in an effort to beat the performance of the benchmark. Index funds, and Exchange Traded Funds are passively managed mutual funds. The fund invests in a particular market index such as the S&P 500 and mirrors the performance of the designated stock or bond index or benchmark. A particular advantage of using passively managed index funds and exchange-traded funds are the lower expense ratios.

Money Market Funds are mutual funds that invest in short-term bonds. They typically pay better interest rates than a savings account, but not as much as a certificate of deposit (CD). The objective of the fund varies with the type of mutual fund. A fund that focuses on stability aims to preserve the principal, while funds focused on growth are targeting increased value of the principal over time.

A traditional Individual Retirement Account (IRA) is a personal savings plan that gives tax advantages for savings for retirement. Investments may include a variety of securities. Contributions are tax-deductible; earnings are not taxed until distributed. A Roth IRA (funded with money that has already been taxed) is a personal savings plan where earnings that remain in the account are not taxed. Investments may include a variety of securities. Contributions are not tax-deductible.

To learn more about managing money:

- American Savings Education Council: http://www.choosetosave.org/asec/
- Investopedia: http://www.investopedia.com/wealth-management/
- The Investor's Clearinghouse: http://www.investoreducation.org/
- MyMoney.gov: http://www.mymoney.gov/Pages/default.aspx

What are some of the investments you would want to be in if you won the lottery? Consult with your financial advisor for specific investment advice tailored to your financial situation. If you haven't yet obtained a financial advisor and have a sudden windfall you can always put money into CDs and/or short-term treasury bills. Use products like CDARs to take advantage of FDIC protection while shopping for and vetting a financial advisor. Also consider brokerage accounts to hold money while making important decisions.

Most importantly don't buy anything or invest into anything that you don't understand. Invest in appreciating assets that have the potential to increase in value and produce income. As you gain knowledge of your wealth and confidence in making financially lucrative decisions, you can consider the following:

- Investing in collectibles, art, and rare gems.
- Options, commodities, futures contracts, hedge funds.
- Real estate, Real Estate Investment Trusts (REITs)
- Buying an entire sports team (NFL, NBA, MLB) or being part of an investment group that buys a sports team.
- Funding Angel rounds for tech startups. Angels secure capital for startups and the average startup needs $1.1m in capital.
- Buying a franchise, McDonalds, Burger King, Chick-fil-A

What Not to do When You Win The Lottery is the second title released in *The Create Your Money Series.* Each title deals specifically with financial topics and information that motivates wealth creation. My books are designed to be quick-reads…. I'm giving you the streamlined, absolutely essential information you need to know, in order to create the money you want, and change your life. I wish you *complete* success on your journey to manage and maintain sudden wealth and on building a wealthy foundation brick-by-brick!

Before you go, I want to thank you for taking the time to buy and read my book. There are dozens of other personal finance books you could have chosen, but you took a chance on me. I'm thrilled that you read this book all the way to the end and I hope that you got a lot out of it. If you liked what you've read then I need your help.... please take a moment to leave a review for this book on Amazon.

Your feedback helps me to continue writing the kind of books that help you create your money and change your world. If you think this information is worth sharing, please take a few seconds to tell your friends on Facebook and Twitter. If it helps them keep more money in their pocket they'll be grateful to you and so will I!

Follow the link below to leave a review on Amazon:

https://www.amazon.com/dp/B01H0YVVHE

If you have any questions feel free to visit my website and leave a comment on one of the articles or drop me a line. Sign up for my email list to receive the latest information through my newsletters, classes and events!

http://www.AngelLovesMoney.com

https://www.facebook.com/AngelLuvsMoney/

follow us on twitter

@AngelLuvsMoney

58582985R00080

Made in the USA
Charleston, SC
13 July 2016